Super
Strategist

Super Strategist

The Art and Science of Modern Account Planning

LESLEY BIELBY

FOREWORD BY DOUGLAS ATKIN

Figure.1
Vancouver / Berkeley

Cataloguing data is available from Library and Archives Canada
ISBN 978-1-77327-147-7 (hbk.)
ISBN 978-1-77327-148-4 (ebook)
ISBN 978-1-77327-149-1 (pdf)

Jacket design by Jessica Sullivan and Naomi MacDougall
Interior design by Naomi MacDougall
Front jacket image by nicomenijes/iStockphoto.com
Author photograph by Jeremy Ramirez

Editing by Michael Leyne
Copy editing by Jennifer D. Foster
Proofreading by Alison Strobel

Printed and bound in Canada by Friesens
Distributed internationally by Publishers Group West

Figure 1 Publishing Inc.
Vancouver BC Canada
www.figure1publishing.com

For Archie, Iona, and Euan

"If it doesn't sell, it isn't creative."

—DAVID OGILVY

Contents

FOREWORD BY DOUGLAS ATKIN XI

INTRODUCTION 1

one
An Industry in Flux 5

two
**From Account Planner
to Super Strategist** 11

three
Brand Matters 29

four
The Brand House 43

five
Modern Consumer Research 63

six
**Data and the Science
of Strategic Planning** 89

seven
The Creative Brief 121

eight
The Customer Journey 135

ACKNOWLEDGMENTS 164

Foreword

THOUGHT IT WAS ODD, when I arrived in New York from London almost 30 years ago, that many clients and agency colleagues thought that planning was about being "consumer-led." Odd, for two reasons. For many of our clients (and some of the agency people), thinking about the consumer *at all* in the development of the brand was considered to be a huge innovation. They were touting it proudly and glad to have our help. But, it was also odd, because even some of the leaders of this new Brit-import called "account planning" thought that "consumer-led" defined this new discipline. In my view, it doesn't and it never did.

Saying you're "consumer-led" means well. It's trying to put the consumer at the center of your operations. Which, as I mentioned, was a radical idea 30 years ago and a big advance for many companies. But being led by the consumer is a very dangerous idea. It will mean that you will almost always be a follower. You will seldom innovate.

It's much better to be *idea-led, but consumer-informed.*

I'm talking about this in the Foreword to Lesley's excellent and much-needed book, because there's always been the need to balance art and science in the act of branding. But science should always be in the service of ideas. Ideas change things. They disrupt the status quo and force a change in people's attitudes, beliefs, and behaviors.

This is something we lived daily during the hyper-growth years at Airbnb, as it disrupted not just categories, but also whole economies. Even fundamental human behavior. Apparently, it was a "crazy idea" to trust strangers enough to have them stay in your home. But it was an idea that went from crazy to the new norm, with many disruptions on the way.

The three founders are different from most Silicon Valley types. Two of them—Brian and Joe—were product designers. They have a hunger for big cheeky ideas. Data was there to inform those ideas: to make them less of a leap into the dark and more of a step into the semi-light. The data gave us confidence that this was (probably) the right thing to do. But, ultimately, we knew that a truly good idea was always going to have risk attached.

And that's what makes good planners, in my view. They are there to champion big ideas. And they do it with a conviction that's derived from data that says it's (probably) the right thing to do. But they also do it with the conviction that great ideas make big things happen. Because, after all, if you're not helping make big things happen with a big juicy idea, what's the point?

DOUGLAS ATKIN
Former Global Head of Community & Architect of Purpose,
Culture and Core Values, Airbnb
Author, *The Culting of Brands*
July 2020

Introduction

I N 1999, I crammed myself into a Marriott Hotel conference room with over two thousand other people. Standing room only. Speakers lined up on the front row with notes in clammy hands. We were at one of the earliest Account Planning Group conferences in the United States. The energy was palpable. As everyone settled in to listen to the first speaker, I—and every other person in the room—realized that because of the two thousand souls in this room, the advertising industry in the United States would never again be the same. This was a pivotal moment in our industry. Truly, the beginning of a new and exciting era.

I had been headhunted from the trendy, maverick London hot shop, Howell Henry Chaldecott Lury, 6 months earlier, to bring the discipline of account planning to iconic Southern ad agency, McKinney & Silver. A big Audi of America client meeting had been canceled, and I was curious to see what a room full of American planners looked like, so had decided at the last minute to attend the conference. I have never loved crowded conferences, being somewhat introverted and slightly claustrophobic. But planning was in its infancy in the USA, so I assumed the conference would be small, intimate, low key, and manageable.

I couldn't have been more wrong. Where had these people come from? How was it possible that over two thousand planners could even exist in America already, never mind attend the same conference?

As I worked my way around the room, uncomfortably introducing myself to those in close proximity, I quickly realized that only about a tenth of these people were truly experienced account planners. And most of those were Brits who had crossed the pond before me, bringing the discipline with them. I already knew some of them from the UK, and several were my heroes—they had sought new adventures in the U.S., after making their mark on the industry after many, many years in London agencies.

So, if most weren't already planners, who were they? As it turned out, they were account managers, media planners, researchers, business analysts, and brand consultants. Like moths to a flame, they had smartly noticed the brilliant growth of this important new discipline in other agencies all across North America and had responded by switching hats and quickly learning this new trade—typically, from their new British department heads.

I believed then, and still believe today, that only in America could a craft that had taken over 30 years to develop in the UK be so quickly mastered by a ragtag group of strategic and insightful misfits. Today, this group has become, arguably, the most influential account planning force in the world. And all of this over a short handful of years.

Over 2 decades later, we find ourselves at another pivotal moment, as our industry struggles to stay relevant in the aftermath of three serious crises, the most recent being COVID-19, which forced many of our agencies to their knees at shocking speed.

Over the last decade, in particular, the advertising industry has changed beyond recognition. Account planning, whose original role was to find and use consumer insight to inform stronger creative ideas, has been utterly transformed into a discipline that most of us don't even call account planning anymore. (At our agency, we now call it strategic planning. It can also be called creative strategy, brand strategy, or brand planning. In reference to the early days, I will refer to it as account planning (in Chapters 1 and 2) and will then switch to strategic planning.)

If your agency is still hiring old-school planners whose sole skill set is feeding insights to creatives, that's a good and necessary skill. But if they are unable to "land the plane" and pull those big insights into strategic, data-driven brand and business transformation ideas, they will not survive in today's industry. Being too ethereal is, by far, the single biggest point of frustration and criticism that I hear from clients about these types of planners. And it inevitably results in them being taken off the business and, ultimately, asked to find a role elsewhere. And this has nothing to do with age or experience. I have had planners in their 50s and 60s in my team who have had stronger digital and social skills than planners half their age. It's a question of making a commitment to continuously evolve and grow. Today's strategists need to appreciate the need for both the art and the science of their craft. But it's important that the science doesn't dominate the art. After all, we are a creative industry. Only the correct blend of both will succeed.

Modern account planners are not one-dimensional. Nor are they "T-shaped." To survive in an increasingly complex and competitive industry, they need to be "X-shaped," to borrow a phrase from design thinking. This means that, rather than being highly skilled in only one area, they must have multiple skills that draw from various fields, including social, digital, brand, and connections planning, as well as content strategy, user experience, and media planning skills. The strategic planner continues to represent the consumer and make the work better. It is also our responsibility to ensure that the work "works," by having a strong grasp of data and analytics, being able to analyze the category and business, being able to track cultural shifts and keep an eye on the competitive set, being skilled in brand development, and, importantly, being able to lead customer journey development—all important tools for the modern strategist.

Your agency is falling behind if it is not training and producing multiskilled X-shaped planners who possess all of these skills, as well as the ability to use a plethora of different research methodologies to truly understand the consumer mindsets, attitudes, and behaviors.

It sounds like a lot and it is. But it's essential for the well-being of any contemporary agency—and to ensure a bright future for each planner. Earlier white papers and books claimed that advertising never *needed* account planning. While it may have added something extra that had value, it was not critical. Perhaps that used to have some degree of truth to it. Today, however, clients often demand account planners more than all other roles, except creative (quite rightly). I firmly believe that as account planning has become more of a strategic function, it has become absolutely essential.

In the following pages, I will, as simply and directly as possible (I am not and never will be an academic), share my experiences as a 30-year veteran of the advertising industry, a working chief strategy officer whose career spans the history of the discipline—from the extreme highs, to the brink of obscurity, and back again—across two continents and four cities.

The first chapter tells how it all began—first in the UK and then in the USA—and shares the story of my own start in the industry, and the digital and social explosions that changed everything. The rest of the book will focus on the tools of the account planners' trade—both traditional and new—as well as insights into the quickly evolving industry that I chose to make my life's work. I will also offer suggestions on how to, as an account planner or strategic planner, stay relevant, stay ahead, and stay interested in this exciting, sometimes exasperating, and always interesting career path.

I wrote this book primarily for all of those young would-be or current account planners and strategists who have asked me for recommendations over the years—because I got weary of suggesting book titles that were extremely outdated or too academic. Perhaps what I have learned over my long career to date will provide some helpful guidance. I hope you find this book useful, and that it helps you understand the role a modern X-shaped strategic planner—a Super Strategist—can play in helping build and transform your clients' business.

one

An Industry in Flux

WHEN PEOPLE ASK what I do for a living, I feel an odd sense of discomfort saying, "I work in advertising." Why? Because it feels dated. It feels perhaps even weirder to explain, "I work at an *ad agency*." I know they're picturing Don Draper in a snappy suit, cigarette and TV storyboards in hand, and not the latest trending Instagram Stories or TikTok posts.

To understand the modern account planner and their equally modern tool kit, let's first ground ourselves by taking a look at the changes in their natural environment—today's advertising agency and the brands they promote.

The word "advertising" carries not only the negative baggage of the *Mad Men* era, but also the implication that it's a one-way street— me, the slick marketer, pitching to you, the unsuspecting consumer. "Advertising" implies that one is advertised *to* versus engaged *with*. As anyone in today's industry knows, the idea of talking to (or, rather, *at*) people to sell them something has gone the way of the rotary phone. The consumer has never been more sophisticated or better prepared to fend off unwanted messages with ad blocking. Appointment viewing? You may as well show up at their door with a case full of encyclopedias.

So, what is the right word these days? For those of you in the industry, I'm sure you have sat in client meetings where everyone avoided the dilemma by talking about "communications" and "content," instead of "advertising." We don't talk about "TV" but, instead, refer to "video." (But ignore the rumors that TV is dying—the context of TV has changed but it remains strong, even if we do now call it "video.") With print almost dead, radio declining, and digital and social seeing meteoric growth, is this still an advertising industry? What does the word "advertise" even mean? Let's consult the lexico.com definition:

ad·ver·tise · /ˈadvətʌɪz/

verb

1. describe or draw attention to (a product, service, or event) in a public medium in order to promote sales or attendance.

Take a deep breath—advertising is simply drawing attention to a product to promote action. So, isn't what we do today still advertising? I believe it is.

What has changed is the sheer quantity of media, channels, and platforms at our disposal. We now spend several hours every day on our phone, looking at apps and websites stuffed with messaging, much of it irrelevant. Advertising and brands are everything and everywhere now—not just traditional channels, but also every single potential consumer touchpoint and experience. That is what makes it so hard to engage people and pull them in.

Our limited attention spans make it even more difficult. In the 1960s, when media channels were scant and fewer brands existed, you could trust that if you put an ad out there in a TV show, most of the audience would get the same impression. And if it were a popular program, like *The Andy Griffith Show*, then you knew that a huge proportion of the population experienced the same brand exposure and would later have similar brand recall.

Over the last couple decades or so, as the media landscape has fragmented beyond recognition, advertisers have at times acted like petulant toddlers, stamping our feet for attention. You may remember the (ultimately, banned) ad for Cyberian Outpost from the beginning of the dot-com era, which showed and literally coined the phrase "shooting gerbils out of a cannon"?

At our best, however, we have created content that is so rich and compelling that it made old, stodgy brands famous again in record time. A great example is the relaunch of the aging brand Old Spice. The "Smell Like a Man, Man" campaign by Wieden+Kennedy launched at the 2010 Super Bowl and set social media on fire, quickly racking up 40 million YouTube views. Did it work? Within 30 days of the campaign launch, sales of Old Spice bodywash increased 107 percent. You bet it worked.

But this campaign ran over a decade ago, when things were a lot simpler. The attention of today's consumer must be earned. It is more important than ever for advertisers to create authentic interactions. We can't just bait the consumer; we need to offer something of value. Something they *choose* to spend time with and even seek out. Something unexpected that provides a connection that is not just a one-way street, but also a freeway of valuable information and useful ideas.

To that end, it has been impossible for account planning to stand still. So, how has it evolved? Who is the modern account planner, and what role should they play in our industry today? Let's start at the beginnings.

A Tale of Two Beginnings

In 1964, Stephen King, of acclaimed London ad agency J. Walter Thompson (JWT), was deeply frustrated. His teams were developing advertising with little or no consumer input, resulting in ineffective campaigns for his clients.

Four years later, Stanley Pollitt of the equally acclaimed BMP London grew concerned for similar reasons. His account management department was not using any data or consumer research to provide rigor and inspiration to their creative briefs. He began to suspect what we all know to be true today: great briefs are much more likely to result in famous and effective advertising that benefits not only agencies, but, critically, also their clients.

Because King and Pollitt believed that "the empty chair" (the consumer) was not being represented during campaign development, each independently developed a new and exciting advertising agency discipline, one that focused entirely on the consumer's relationship with brands and advertising, and brought together skills and insights from disciplines like media planning, research, brand consulting, and account management. In the mid-1960s, account planning was born.

Almost 2 decades later, in 1982, Jay Chiat of Chiat\Day noticed this new discipline. Chiat already believed that British creative ideas were generally stronger than American ideas, and he decided to make the historic move of hiring Jane Newman, a British account planner, to develop the role to fit within his already successful New York agency, inspiring better, more effective work. His experiment succeeded beyond his dreams—within a decade, Chiat\Day's annual billings shot up from $50 million to $700 million, proving that account planning, when done well, can be a game changer. It didn't take long for the rest of the world to catch on, with most agencies across most continents adopting account planning quickly and effectively by importing their own "British planner" to spearhead the approach.

From the 1970s through to the mid-1990s (pre-Internet), account planning's role was relatively simple. The planning cycle, as defined by Stephen King in 1974 (see page 9), was more or less fixed. With chart in hand, the actions required by the account planner to complete the cycle were:

1. attend the client briefing

2. identify the key target audience (within a tight demographic range)

3. identify the current situation and desired outcome

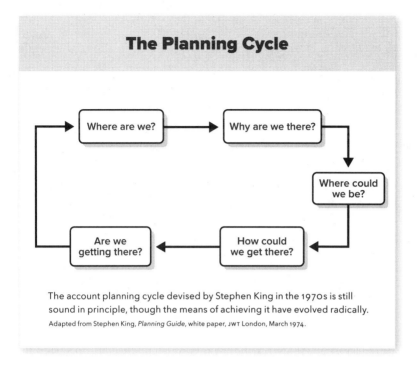

The Planning Cycle

Where are we? → Why are we there? → Where could we be?

Are we getting there? ← How could we get there? ←

The account planning cycle devised by Stephen King in the 1970s is still sound in principle, though the means of achieving it have evolved radically.

Adapted from Stephen King, *Planning Guide*, white paper, JWT London, March 1974.

4. conduct consumer research (qualitative/focus groups, typically)

5. use insights from that research to inform the creative brief

6. brief the creatives

7. stand back and wait for creatives to develop campaign ideas

8. make sure the work is "on brief" and not just a great idea, for art's sake

9. sometimes, but not always, test the creative ideas to improve their effectiveness. (Although, this testing often had the opposite effect, of killing on-brief, innovative ideas that scared consumers to death. More on that later.)

10. help account management and creatives by preselling the idea to clients, to help defend the work via the evidence of positive consumer sentiment

11. stand back and hope that the ad worked (the KPI—key performance indicator—was typically an increase in sales, which was often hard to determine)

A talented and intuitive account planner would show empathy with the intended audience and make the work more relevant. The idea would then be stronger and more likely to emerge from the painful process of copy testing relatively unscathed and survive the inevitable layers of client approval. By the time I entered the London advertising industry in 1990, each agency, with few exceptions, had a robust account planning department that played a pivotal role in the development of effective work.

These basic principles continue to be the foundation of good planning, though the practice has evolved tremendously, almost beyond recognition. The duopoly of Google and Facebook has swallowed up the majority of today's online ad market, and when it comes to convenience, scale, and, of course, consumer data, ad agencies cannot begin to compete with the cookie monsters. This isn't necessarily a question of one industry replacing another, as has been heavily reported, but more about agencies working in collaboration with tech companies. The process is now more integrated, less linear, and more complex, demanding multiple skills across digital, social, and brand strategy.

In addition, despite the huge and important proliferation of technologies like machine learning and artificial intelligence (AI), we have to remember that the human brain has always been composed of two, not just one, parts. Modern planners and modern agencies need to use every tool and technology (and data partner) at their disposal and also provide something that is not purely algorithm based—and much harder to replicate. And that is the intangible but powerful strategic and creative human elements.

two

From Account Planner to Super Strategist

MY OWN ENTRANCE into the discipline was unconventional. After university I taught English in a business school in Paris for 2 years. I returned to the UK penniless and decided to try temping, despite my dubious typing skills.

(When I was in high school in Paisley, Scotland, typing classes were required for girls. I was one of the worst typists in my year. I tell myself today that my incompetence was a deliberate act of rebellion, fueled by my great offense at the assumption that few of the female graduates would have any career beyond working in a typing pool. Little did I know that this would be the most useful of any classes I took in high school.)

My first assignment was at an ad agency called Collett, Dickenson, Pearce and Partners (CDP), which was situated on Euston Road in London. The CDP building was a 1970s block (that later became a hotel), with white walls and trendy 90s black ash furniture. It was full of dapper old white men with nice suits and posh accents, such as John Ritchie, who ran the Benson & Hedges cigarette business

11

(John's son Guy later became a famous film director). But there were enough young, attractive people working there to pique my interest, and I was also impressed by the fact that many creative celebrities had passed through CDP, including Charles Saatchi, Ridley Scott, Alan Parker, and David Puttnam. What I did not know or appreciate back then is that I had been very, very lucky with where I had landed. I had stumbled into one of the most creative agencies in not only London, but also the world.

After 3 weeks in my role of new-business assistant, John Ritchie's secretary, Felicity, who was willing to do anything to get away from my awful typing, suggested a job that involved more hands-on work. I became a traffic assistant, reporting to Paul Adams, CDP's head of traffic. Traffic's job was to manage a timetable and get ads through the system by asking (or, more typically, forcing) each individual department head to sign off on every creative brief, script, copy, piece of artwork, mechanical (mock-up ads), and finished ad. This rigorous quality control has more or less disappeared from our industry. However, I believe that it played a vital role. Having heads of account management, planning, art, copy, and, most importantly, creative directors control the quality of the brief and the work meant that it became significantly stronger. It also, however, made the job of being a traffic assistant very difficult. A year in traffic was a brilliant way to learn how ads get made. Importantly, it also helped me develop a thick skin: countless moody creatives yelled at me when I reminded them their copy or artwork was due. As a young person new to a volatile industry, I quickly learned that creative people did not really like sticking to a timetable. (They still don't.)

After my tenure in traffic, I was given the opportunity to jump onto the prestigious CDP graduate training program, which was already in full swing. I did my best, juggling it with my full-time job, and learned a lot about the industry and the agency. Most importantly, during the program I got to know Richard Swaab, head of planning (and now deputy chairman, AMV BBDO, London). He didn't have to work too hard to convince me that account planning was a viable career route for me, because of my love of brilliant creative, street smarts, and natural sense of curiosity and intuition.

Richard took pity on me after a lot of whining and let me write my first creative brief for a new client, The Rainforest Foundation. The objective of the campaign was to raise money to save the South American rainforests and prevent the genocide of the Indigenous peoples in that region, particularly the Yanomami, the tribe that had been most affected.

My first real client was—unapologetic name-drop here—Sting. He and his wife, Trudie Styler, were diligent about the work they were doing for The Rainforest Foundation, and he often visited the agency to brief us and review work. After our very first meeting, he asked me if we could get some food, as he had skipped lunch. I offered to take him to the CDP canteen (I can't believe I actually did that) and, remarkably, he said yes. In the course of our lunch, two female employees who had clapped eyes on him promptly fainted. But as glamorous and famous as he was, we were keen to be diligent, too.

Writing that brief for The Rainforest Foundation is when I fell in love with advertising and with account planning. It was when I decided that this is what I wanted to do for the rest of my working life.

My first attempt was clumsy. The terrifying but brilliant creative director John O'Donnell and his somewhat kinder partner, Garry Horner, rejected the brief and threw me out of their office. "This is crap!" John yelled, as he crumpled up the brief and tossed it out the door after me. It bounced off my head.

I had a restless night but showed up outside Garry and John's door again the next morning, with a new and, I hoped, better brief. I had admittedly received some help. A senior planner at the agency had taken pity on me and urged me to focus on an imperative: "Where is the call to action? What will happen if people do not donate?" I gave him a vague and rambling answer. He asked me to simplify. Twice.

I eventually mumbled, "The rainforests will no longer exist, and the Yanomami will die."

"Perfect," he said. So, that's what I put in the brief.

As I stood outside John and Garry's office door, knees shaking, their secretary, Kitty, threw me a pitying look. I also held a second offering—a copy of *Bury My Heart at Wounded Knee*, by Dee Brown, which is a devastatingly heartbreaking biography about the genocide

Imagine a fire stretching from London to Athens.

The smoke is so thick that aircraft cannot land.

The heat so intense that trees nowhere near the inferno suddenly buckle and burst into flames.

Ancient hardwoods, tough as steel, are incinerated within minutes.

So fierce is the destruction, so all-consuming, that by the time you finish this page, one hundred acres of tropical forest will be gone.

Forever.

This may sound like the apocalyptic fantasy of a new disaster movie, but it is all too real.

On 28th September, 1987 a satellite of the National Oceanographic and Atmospheric Administration photographed such a fire.

A fire, that on closer examination, was made up of 5,000 individual fires.

While this is deeply disturbing, more alarming is the fact that it is not unusual.

Between July and September, it is the burning season in Amazonia.

The Goddard Space Flight Center in Maryland, again with the help of satellite pictures, estimates that a total of 240,000 fires rage during these months.

When they are eventually doused by the onset of torrential rains, a shroud of fine grey ash covers an area the size of England, Scotland and Wales.

So far, more than 40 million acres of the Brazilian Amazon have been destroyed.

Only now, after twenty years of burning, is the world waking up to the idea that we are attacking one of our most valuable life support systems.

Besides being the hub of a rainfall cycle that supplies water to around one billion people, these forests feed us and heal us.

An average of one in four purchases from western high street chemists contain compounds derived from rainforest species.

They provide us with 70% of the three thousand plants identified by the US National Cancer Institute as having cancer fighting properties. Vincristine, for example, a lifesaver in the treatment

TWO WORKS OF MAN ARE VISIBLE FROM SPACE. THE GREAT WALL OF CHINA AND THE FIRES RAGING IN THE RAINFOREST.

of childhood leukaemia, is donated by the rosy periwinkle.

Rice, maize, peanuts, avocado, citrus fruits, pineapple, cocoa, coffee, tea and sugar all come from the rainforests.

Yet this is a mere taste of how bountiful the harvest could be.

The Kayapo Indians of central Brazil collect fruit from no fewer than 250 trees, plants and shrubs.

While at least 1,650 known tropical plants have potential as vegetable crops.

How much more is waiting to be discovered?

How much has already been lost as species of plant and flower, insect and butterfly, bird and animal, reptile and amphibian, disappear at the rate of one every half hour?

As if this is not tragic enough, a greater tragedy lies in the fate of the indigenous people.

Of the tribes that roamed those great forests at the turn of the century, more than one third have disappeared.

Murdered, poisoned, decimated by white man's diseases, driven from their lands and hounded to extinction.

Today fewer than 200,000 Indians remain.

Yet within this fragile community lies the only hope for the future of the rainforests. These are the traditional lands of the Indians.

But what they need now is help to battle with the alien concepts of property and ownership.

Help to secure and enforce the demarcation of their territories.

And help to protect themselves against the violation of their human rights. It was with these objectives, that the Rainforest Foundation was established in 1988.

We're now at work in twelve countries worldwide with our principal strength in Brazil.

Here, our team is made up of eminent anthropologists, lawyers specialising in indigenous land rights and Indian leaders.

They are unpaid (we are a voluntary organisation) dedicated and highly qualified.

Between them, they have devised schemes, ideas and projects to protect the Indians and preserve the forests.

What the Foundation desperately needs is funds to implement them.

The race, as ever, is against time.

Last summer, Raoni, a Kayapo chief, went on a world tour to draw attention to the plight of his people.

When he spoke of his home, he said this: "My spirit is always warning me that when the forest is all destroyed there will be very strong winds. The sun will get very hot. It will be difficult to breathe. Then everybody will die. Not just the Indians. I am warning you. You have to think. You have to change your ideas. Leave the jungle alone."

In thirty days time, the fires will begin again.

Please send your donations to: The Rainforest Foundation, Mullerbuoy Johnson, Marvic House, Bishops Road, London SW6 7AD. Cheques should be made payable to "The Rainforest Foundation." Please enclose an SAE if you require acknowledgement of receipt or further information.

Name:

Address:

THE RAINFOREST FOUNDATION

Copywriter JOHN O'DONNELL Art Director GARRY HORNER Photographer ALASDAIR OGILVIE

This ad, from a 1990-91 campaign for The Rainforest Foundation, was created from my first creative brief. The campaign spurred significant donations to fight the deforestation of the Amazon rainforest, won several awards for our agency, and set me on a lifelong career path.

Featured in John Salmon and John Ritchie, *Inside Collett Dickenson Pearce* (London: B.T. Batsford, 2001).

of Indigenous peoples in North America, in particular in the late 19th century. I had finished the book two nights before and hadn't stopped thinking about it. It seemed to me the plight of the Yanomami was history repeating itself, and I thought this book might be useful for my meeting with the creatives. I hoped that each of my offerings would please and inspire them.

I feebly knocked at the door, handed over the brief and the book, and stepped back. I had no idea that I was actually supposed to brief them (and I would have been too scared and shy to do so, anyway). I stood and waited. After a few gut-wrenching minutes, John looked at me and said, "Yeah, this is okay."

Beaming from ear to ear, I turned to leave. Garry, however, was determined not to let me get *too* pleased with myself. He yelled after me, "There are two of us, and you only brought one book." I happily skipped off to WHSmith to spend my pathetic salary on another copy.

One ad that John and Garry created featured the headline "Genocide 1890" above an image of an Indigenous North American chief. Below it was a similar image, but of a Yanomami chief, above the words "Genocide 1990." A second ad featured a burnt tree, twisted into a shape reminiscent of Jesus on the cross. The print campaign helped raise awareness of the plight of the Yanomami, as well as a decent sum of money for The Rainforest Foundation. It also won several prestigious awards.

I hadn't written these ads but I felt the glowing pride of seeing my work in them—even if only a little. This is one of the most euphoric feelings an account planner can experience. It is like a drug, because you are constantly chasing that high. It is what drives you to keep going. It has kept me going for 30 years and still does to this day.

The Painful Process of Introducing Account Planning to a U.S. Agency

After 10 years in the London advertising industry, I received a call from a headhunter who told me that some of her U.S.-based clients were looking for senior planners to start up the discipline at their agencies. After a few rounds of interviews, I was hired by Don Maurer, new CEO of McKinney & Silver, to introduce account planning to that agency for the first time. By 1999 the logic of employing account planning in any agency was clear. But that didn't mean it was always embraced with open arms by agency staff.

McKinney was a legacy Southern agency with a rich history of famous print creative, much of it groundbreaking. By the end of the 20th century, however, their reel had weakened and the agency was losing relevance. Their best work was from the era when a hunch and a handshake were enough to launch a campaign. Now, competition in most categories was intense. Clients were more demanding. They wanted work that stood out and they wanted more rigor. More discipline. More evidence that the insights into the consumer were correct and the idea would sell product. This made sense in principle, but McKinney (and the industry, in general) had overcorrected towards more left-brain, turgid, client-dominated briefs that made the creative too rational. They weren't finding the balance between art and science. The work wasn't working, and clients had left without being replaced. McKinney was shrinking. Something had to change.

Don knew that to turn around the agency, they needed a new approach, and new talent was vital. So, he hired a whole new leadership team. That included me and the talented new executive creative director (ECD), David Baldwin, who, in turn, had started to hire some brilliant teams: most notably, art director Philip Marchington and copywriter Jean Rhode. Thankfully, they both had experience with, and were fans of, account planning.

Don was excited to bring a young Scottish planner across the pond from London. The account people at McKinney, on the other hand, were instantly suspicious of me. Why? Because it quickly became apparent that planning took the fun out the process for them. Prior to my arrival, in addition to their responsibilities for managing clients, they had commissioned and attended, or even moderated, the focus groups. They wrote the creative briefs and had the primary relationships with the creative teams. They did not want to give up those things, which was understandable. But the agency was no longer producing award-winning work, and new business opportunities were scant.

It was important to me that I win over the account management department. To do this, I had to position planning as neither a threat nor a killjoy, but as an ally that would help make the work better. Because here is the most important thing that I want you to take out from this book. It was important decades ago and it is equally important today:

When the work is good, everything is good.

Good work wins awards and attracts better talent. In particular, creative talent. Better talent means better work. Good work gets noticed and talked about by consumers. It increases sales. An increase in sales and a famous campaign make clients happy, because it makes their bosses happy (and because some of the fame rubs off on all of them). This makes them more inclined to stick with the agency, or even throw them more brands to work on. Famous work is noticed by consultants and other clients, who want some of that magic for themselves—so, the agency wins more new business, becomes more successful, hires even better talent . . . and so it goes. Bottom line? I repeat:

When the work is good, everything is good.

After reviewing a few agency creative briefs, it became abundantly clear that while factually accurate, most were not inspiring. There was no clear single proposition. They were too long, with too much information. They were stuffed like sausages. Any experienced account planner would have known that they would not help the creatives get to good and effective work.

To prove that account planning could help make the work better—for the good of everyone—I decided to focus on one initial project. The agency hadn't won any significant pitches for some time. With the new leadership team, chief marketing officers (CMOs) and consultants had taken notice of the new McKinney & Silver, and two pitch RFPs soon came through the door. The first was Aetna, and the second was very exciting—Disaronno Amaretto. It was time to get to work.

For the Disaronno pitch, I attached myself to the lead pitch creatives, Philip and Jean, and they, in turn, did the same. The creative team even refused to attend pitch meetings unless planning was there, which I much appreciated. As an integrated team, we decided to pitch differently—with a high degree of collaboration and discipline. We analyzed the client problems in depth. I led a fresh approach to consumer research that was informed by the whole team. I wrote a concise and crisp creative brief, and the pitch team gave valuable input. The creatives came up with many great ideas, and we sifted through them together. We worked in lockstep and we kept it simple, clear, and inclusive. We also made it fun.

The single proposition from the creative brief was one short phrase that represented the absolute essence of Disaronno Amaretto. It would revitalize this tired brand, leading consumers from their current impression—"a sickly, old-fashioned almond-flavored liqueur that I drink infrequently"—to where we wanted them to be:

> Disaronno Amaretto is a warm, modern elixir
> that ignites the senses.

This brief inspired a totally immersive customer experience, from velvet ropes, to soft, deep red fabric–covered bar stools; soft bar mats with sexy slogans; exotic, sensual cocktail recipes; and beautiful multisensory bar staff kits. Don Maurer somehow convinced Ben & Jerry's (another client of ours at the time) to create a one-off Disaronno Amaretto ice cream for the clients to try at the pitch. Unbelievable.

All of this was a radical departure from the focus on traditional TV, outdoor, and print of that time. The work was brilliant. The clients agreed, and we won the pitch. Then to top it all, we won Aetna, a significantly bigger brand, using a similar approach.

I will be eternally grateful to the leadership, creatives, and, in fact, everyone, at McKinney & Silver for ultimately embracing and championing account planning. Our collaboration set the foundation for a long and successful stretch for McKinney, as a planning- and creative-led agency.

All Change—The Start of the Digital Age

I was sitting in a gray room, around a gray table, with two employees of CKS (at the time, McKinney's parent company) and one of the founders of a famous big-box store. (I still don't know why on earth I was there.) The founder's pen was poised above a contract, while the CKS guys, who were half his age, literally yelled at him to sign the agency agreement "right now!" so they could secure his domain name before someone else did and get his website up and running. This was at the time when smart people were buying up big brand domain names and selling them to the companies for huge profits. It was in those few seconds I realized this thing called the "Internet" was about to change everything.

The founder signed, and the site was secured. But what I had witnessed had clearly been a power shift that was taking place in this and thousands of other boardrooms. The innovators and early adopters of the Internet were about to rule the world, and the old systems of corporate hierarchy would be destroyed.

In the early to mid-2000s, digital expert companies like Sweden's Hyper Island blew into the U.S. advertising scene and kicked up a terror—of irrelevance and oblivion—in the previously successful traditionalists in our fast-changing industry. Seasoned ECDs resigned in fear. Old-school CEOs were kicked to the curb. Art directors over 40 cried into their light boxes. It became clear that we all had to adapt or disappear into the sunset.

Hyper Island brought the fear. But the ad industry brought the stupidity. First, by commanding that "we are all digital now" and then by instantly proceeding to dismiss every proven technique and approach that had come before. Second, most agencies (except the new, digital-native ones) introduced digital by building micro-agencies within the agency, then unleashed them on the traditional agencies often a year or more later, when they "were ready." Of course, chaos ensued, as the body rejected the new organ.

For traditional ad agencies, this was all a bit of a shock. However, all the chaos and disruption distracted from a real opportunity— digital was an amazing new channel and a fantastic new way to get insight about consumer mindsets and behaviors, and would totally redefine the meaning and definition of advertising and creativity.

Hindsight is always perfect. But our industry would be much further along today had we immediately fused each new digital employee to each traditional discipline or department. Digital strategy would have joined my team of brand planners, for example. Had we done this, we would have been more or less fully integrated 6–7 years ago, instead of being in the situation we're in now, where many agencies, remarkably, are still scrambling to do so. More on that later.

Social Media–All Change Again

When social media became ubiquitous in the early 2010s, our industry immediately recognized that social was a platform for change, as President Obama's campaign had proven in 2008. Social media was a way for massive groups of people to communicate with one another for good (or otherwise). For groups to come together and make a huge impact on our culture. From an advertising perspective, social media also gave us new ways to track consumer behavior, to understand what was important to thousands or even millions of people—not just a few focus group participants. And it introduced the now-popular term "purpose-driven brands."

Social media allowed companies to engage directly with their customers. Brands that did not have a clear and authentic vision and that did not practice honesty and transparency were immediately "outed" by consumers, who would punish them by withdrawing their loyalty and their dollars. The new platforms meant that our industry could find real-time insights from social listening and use those to create relevant and personalized content that people actually wanted and sought out. Then we could conduct real-time in-market testing to track the success of individual ideas, all with relative ease.

Digital and social media injected energy into our industry. They were and still are a gift. But they came with a price. The overwhelming number of channels available today, and the equally overwhelming amount of content that fills them, has created an overabundance of choice and information—much of it from unreliable sources—which can be paralyzing. This particularly applies to younger digital and social media natives, who have never known a life before cell phones, the Internet, and social media.

At its worst, social media can be addictive and destructive, exacting a toll on the mental health of young people. While conducting some global client research on Generation Z (those born between 1996 and 2015), I was short a few U.S. respondents and decided to interview my own children. When asked to talk about the pros and cons of social media, my teenage daughter, Iona, told me that "with social media, you create personas that are not based on reality, and maintaining those personas is overwhelming and exhausting." She might as well have scooped my heart out with a spoon.

Her insight led me to launch a robust national survey on Gen Z by my decision science team at Hill Holliday. The survey results confirmed our fears—at least 55 percent of Gen Zers felt overwhelmed by social media. A similar number believed that social apps, Instagram, in particular, contributed towards their anxiety and depression.

When we released these results to the press in 2017, it was clear that we had hit a nerve. For a decade, social media had been presented as an important vehicle for good (which it can still be; think about how social media channels kept all of us informed and connected through the trauma of the COVID-19 crisis). The negative effects of social media have since been well documented, but just a few short years ago it was a shocking revelation. When the currency for popularity isn't based on how many real friends you have, but on how many likes your latest Instagram post received, it is easy to lose sight of what is authentic and become racked with self-doubt and debilitatingly lowered self-esteem.

Our PR department calculated that the report and the additional content that had sprung from it had brought approximately $3 million of free PR to the agency. We have never had such a successful press launch since. But for all its problems, used diligently, social media continues to be an incredibly important and valuable channel for our industry and our clients.

Strategic Foundations

Twenty years since my adventure introducing account planning to an American agency, today I am the chief strategy officer of a large agency. Account planning has seen a lot of change in a few years. Even the name "account planner" has always been somewhat of a misnomer, so 10 years ago, we at Hill Holliday changed the name of the discipline to "strategist" or "strategic planning," which is how I will refer to it from this point onwards.

The challenge now isn't to prove the value of strategic planning, but working hard to evolve my discipline at the speed of change in our industry. I'm also a manager of 40 people, and it is my responsibility to ensure that my strategists are set up for success now and in the future. I know that X-shaped Super Strategists will be in high demand throughout their entire careers. Plus, evolving towards an X-shaped model has been critical for the future success of our agency.

As I mentioned before, larger agencies in our industry had originally built digital and social departments in silos. These silos were essentially digital and social mini-agencies, with their own strategists, creatives, and producers—the mirror image of their traditional counterparts. It took a long time for many of us to integrate the social, digital, and traditional disciplines, because many of the social and digital natives had multiple skills. In some cases, one person was strategist, creative and producer, and media planner and buyer, all in one. Small agencies can have multidisciplined individuals. It makes them nimbler and more economical. But to truly excel in any modern agency and be an expert in your field, a strategist should be a strategist, and a creative should be a creative, regardless of their background in traditional, digital, or social.* These groups do need to have integrated skills.

Three years ago, on my return to Hill Holliday, after a 5-year gap where I worked for smaller, boutique agencies, and after almost a decade of separation, we finally integrated almost anyone with the title "strategist" into my department. (The exceptions being media

---

* From this point onwards, to keep things simple, when I refer to "creative" I am referring to every discipline that produces some kind of content, from TV to social media to technology.

planning/strategy and content strategy, as these are different skill sets—though, content did recently join my team as a specialized group.) Integration was not easy for us, nor is it easy for any large agency—we had to pick apart a decade-old structure and rebuild it carefully, while holding on to our best talent. All social, digital, content, business, and brand strategists joined my team and report to me. We integrated my proprietary research team with our media agency's data and analytics (D&A) team, renamed the combined team "decision science," and, again, moved them over to join my team of strategists. We also created a discipline within my department that was relatively new to the agency world: business strategy. This discipline analyzes business dynamics and data to help with the up-front part of the data loop (see "Business Analysis," page 97, in Chapter 6). To be a strategic planner on my team, you have to actually be a strategist, as obvious as that sounds, and through interviews we discovered that a handful of people were really not truly "strategic." Those people moved into other departments or left the agency. The X-shaped approach was then extended to the remaining committed strategic planners in my department: each of them, including some who had been traditional or brand strategists for many years, was asked to pick *one* major and *two* minor areas of focus from among traditional, digital, and social. All were expected to have a fourth strategy skill, typically, a basic knowledge of communications or connections planning, so they could be strong partners on our media team. Skills in content, customer experience, and media planning were also important. I knew that the strategic planners would not fully integrate overnight. It would take time—a few years, I believed—to get there. To me, this was a good start and a fair and reasonable way for each strategist to learn the different flavors of strategy over time.

Then something unexpected happened. Most of the social and digital strategists in my team decided that they wanted to pick traditional/brand strategy as their majors, and social and digital as their minors. Wow. I did not see that coming.

Three years on, these fully X-shaped strategic planners have succeeded far, far beyond my expectations. They have picked up traditional and brand skills much faster than I could have imagined. They, in turn, are passing their digital and social skills onto the traditional/ brand strategists. The latter is a little trickier and takes longer, but we are all on track. The biggest challenge that I have today is how to keep us all current and future-proof, as it would be all too easy to slip backwards. Training and exposure to new tools, technologies, platforms, and approaches are all of critical importance. This is always a work in progress, an essential commitment on the part of myself and the agency.

One other thing. Because the social and digital strategists who chose traditional/brand planning as their major succeeded so quickly, from this point onwards, I decided to only hire social and digital strategists (versus traditional/brand strategists) at the junior level for the foreseeable future. These strategists must be committed to learning how to become X-shaped and must own the character traits that are typical of any great planner or strategist, as outlined in the next section. The objective is to achieve a totally X-shaped strategy department, to ensure that my team continues to serve our agency and our clients in the most innovative, progressive, and productive way possible.

This integration has been, without a doubt, the most successful development of any strategy team I have had the privilege to lead. I am extremely proud of my team members, each and every one of them.

The Traits and Tools of Successful Strategic Planners

If you are new to advertising and are actively trying to find a strategic planning role, you will have learned by now that this is no easy task. There aren't enough jobs to go around and so they are in huge demand. This is not what any young person leaving university wants to hear, and in fact I am sure it is downright irritating. But if you have the talent, the hunger, and the drive, no matter how low the odds are, you will succeed in finding the right role.

For all the young would-be planners and strategists out there, you may be wondering which part of the industry to jump into. Does advertising even hold a future for you?

To me, this is an industry that is not dying or shrinking, but shape-shifting. It's an important distinction, and one that I am very passionate about (and I find it very annoying when I read reports of how agencies are being squashed by tech companies, when the truth is a bit more complicated). Just as the context of TV has changed, the context of advertising has changed. Today, there are so many more options available to you, as a lot of talent and client business have moved around in response to these industry shifts.

You can be a planner in an agency or at a media company, at a tech giant or a consulting firm, or at an in-house agency, such as Calvin Klein's. While some stubbornly traditional agencies have disappeared, many more have rightsized, merged (for example, Wunderman Thompson), been bought (Accenture's purchase of Droga5, for example), or evolved to become modern communications agencies that focus on business and brand solutions, not simply advertising. All of these successful companies use technology and data to track, understand consumer behavior, and micro-target. All work continuously and actively stay ahead of the curve at all times.

However, to survive and thrive, contemporary agencies need to balance logic and creativity. Left and right brain. Technology and humanity. Art and science. If you are more of a left-brain, logical thinker who believes in technology more than anything else, then one of the tech giants may be a more viable option. If you are a very creative person who enjoys breaking convention to create ripples to earn engagement, then being a planner or strategist at an ad agency may be for you.

When you're certain (or as certain as anyone can be in your early to mid-20s) that advertising and strategic planning are what you really want to do, study the industry. Use your networks and ask for informational interviews with planners of all levels. Try to get internships. And, of course, read this book and then decide. If you realize you don't have a passion for the industry, if it isn't something you know you will truly love, move on. Life is too short to not do something that you love.

Once you're committed, all you need is a university degree, ideally, but not necessarily, in media communications or something similar; skills in digital and social media (if you're not a digital and social native, learn fast or pick another career—it is an absolute non-negotiable); and most, if not all, of the following personal and professional qualities, which I have consistently seen in the best planners I have worked with:

· that rare mix of left and right brain—an equal love of art and of science, creative and analytics

· an interesting and/or diverse background—culturally, geographically, or otherwise

· natural curiosity—always trying to understand how things work and why

· intuition—a great planner can hypothesize an outcome and use research to validate or disprove it, but an intuitive planner is rarely completely wrong

· empathy—a proven ability to step into others' shoes

· adaptability and flexibility—while I was at Merkley Newman Harty in New York City, we discovered that 13 of the 16 planners in our department had moved at least 10 times before the age of 16 years (odd, to say the least!)

· cultural literacy—the best planners are enthusiastic early followers of global trends in art, music, film, theater, sport, media, fashion, and popular culture

· a great sense of humor—work is simply better when we can all have a laugh

If you want to work in a full-service agency as a strategic planner, it is important that you seek out a role in an agency that has either fully integrated brand, digital, and social strategy, or one that was founded within the last 10 years or so, as a digital or social agency. Any agency that has not yet integrated is very much behind, and at this point, it will be much harder for them to catch up. If you work in an agency that hasn't yet integrated, help make it happen or move on to a more modern agency that is willing to embrace X-shaped strategic planning. And make sure that the company you are joining is committed to constant evolution or even transformation—otherwise, run for the hills.

Once you've found the right agency and role, what's next? Start planning.

three
Brand Matters

THE MODERN STRATEGIC PLANNER needs a robust and relevant tool kit to rise to the level of Super Strategist. That begins with a strong understanding of the importance of brand and the acquisition of the brand asset development skills we'll discuss in this chapter, so they can protect and nurture brands.

The strategic planners, analysts, and researchers on my team at Hill Holliday are all deeply involved in brand development projects at any given time. This is one of the most important skills a Super Strategist can have. I believe in this so strongly that 3 years ago we launched a brand consultancy called HHBrandAble within my current agency to assist current full-service clients, as well as new project-based clients. I will get into the tools a planner needs to be able to do this kind of work shortly, but let's start with the definition of "brand," again from lexico.com:

brand · /brand/

noun

1. a type of product manufactured by a particular company under a particular name.

The definition of a brand has not changed much over the years. Nor has the role of a brand in contrast to a mere product: a brand still adds value for the consumer and gives the seller the ability to charge a premium, by creating a perception that the product is of superior quality, is more trustworthy, and has a stronger sense of identity that will rub off onto the consumer, and how others perceive *them*. And that, in turn, creates brand preference. Which, if the brand delivers consistently, creates *loyalty*. In essence, a brand is a promise made and kept with a consumer.

For example, most facial moisturizers are made of the same basic ingredients, including glycerin, shea butter, and vitamin E. Written as a list, it is not particularly desirable. But when these ingredients are packaged in a beautiful jar with an appealing brand name and a strong visual identity, and when that package is shown in an advertising campaign that promises youthfulness, vitality, and hope, then it becomes a brand. And consumers will pay much, much more for a brand—especially when it promises something (typically, emotional) they desire and believe they are missing.

Pharmacy stores often place their own-label moisturizers, with absolutely identical ingredients, right next to big brands. They will even add point-of-sale signage, "Compare our ingredients to those found in brand X," to encourage the consumer to pick the cheaper product. Even though the consumer rationally understands that these products are identical, they are still typically driven to purchase the brand version. This defies logic—it's the same tub of ingredients for significantly more money—but the brand offers certainty and the perception that perhaps, somehow, it is superior. Plus, the ad campaign really spoke to them—it made them *feel something* about the brand, something that resonated with their own personal values. Another simple reason for brand choice: many consumers prefer to display the brand name on their bathroom shelf. It says, "I'm not cheap" and "I value myself and I am worth it" more than own-label does (which may be cause to wonder if those who buy own-label have higher self-esteem).

Recent figures show U.S. sales of own-label products are up 15 percent over last year, which may seem like a counter-example.

But there is a simple reason for this that actually reinforces the importance of brands: many of the own-label products are maturing and becoming brands themselves, with their own strong identities, brand assets, and even advertising campaigns. For example, the 80-plus-year-old Boots No7 was a cheap and simple pharmacy store beauty line in the UK and is now—post-partial Walgreens takeover—a premium power brand worth $1 billion globally.

In summary, the stronger the brand, the higher the premium, and the higher the price tag. Brands aren't just "nice to have," nor are they the stuff of "soft marketing metrics." Brands make good business sense. Period.

It's All About the Journey

Where it gets tricky is in understanding exactly what your brand means to consumers, and how to influence that. Why? Well, brand has become complex over the last few years. Imagine midtown Manhattan on a Monday morning (prepandemic). Think of the thousands of people who walk past one another every day. Now think about this: each of these people has a totally different impression of any given brand at the same time. Let's imagine a brand called Sally's Mac and Cheese, for example. Some people have a very clear picture, a well-defined impression of the brand. For others, the image is hazy, but they have some idea of the brand, or a distant memory of the brand. And for many people, there may be no brand impression at all.

The point is, people will have a multitude of different brand impressions at any given time. This will depend on their birthplace, their home, how often they travel, their demographic profile, the psychographic group they belong to, the channels they watch, the social media they use, which search engines they use, their eating habits... the list goes on and on. Suffice to say, we can no longer assume, as we did decades ago, that everyone a) is given the same brand message at the same time; b) consumes those messages at the same time and in the same way; or c) acts upon their impressions of the brand at the same time, or at all. It is just not possible, unless you are an identical twin who has lived alongside your sibling your

Consumer impressions of brands vary from hazy memories to vivid definitions, as illustrated here with our imagined Sally's Mac and Cheese.

entire life, sharing every single experience, each minute of each day, in exactly the same way. It just can't happen.

If consumers' brand impressions are all over the map today, then so is their behavior. So, why do modern brands frequently assume that consumers navigate a category in a straight line? The traditional "purchase funnel" model, as well as the more recent "loyalty loop" or "purchase cycle," assumes they approach a purchase decision predisposed towards certain brands, then use a linear and logical process of decision-making to filter out individual brands until only one choice remains. This perfect triangle and complete, interruption-free circle are truly and completely out of date. Let's agree to put them to rest for good.

Contemporary consumer behavior is much more complicated. Modern consumers are exposed to a large volume and variety of media channels and experience a perpetual state of connectedness. We change our minds constantly. A brand can be seen in a favorable light for decades and then disgrace itself, such as when the over

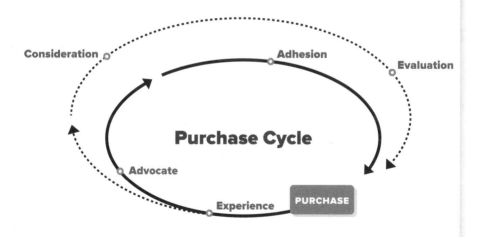

The old-fashioned "purchase funnel" (top) and "purchase cycle" models of consumer behavior assumed an orderly, linear process that isn't relevant in today's chaotic, brand-saturated media landscape.

160-years-old Wells Fargo was fined by regulators in 2016 for creating fake customer accounts. This kind of thing can cause a brand to disappear from our decision-making process, even towards the end of the "funnel" or "loop." Or a new brand launch could pop up in the middle of the decision process, through a favorite celebrity's Instagram post, for example. For larger purchases like luxury apparel or a vehicle, people may even leave the process for 6 months and come back to it out of the blue. Interruptions happen for any number of reasons: a sudden influx of cash, a new job, a new partner, a desire to change their image.

Many unique events influence a consumer on their way to a purchase. They may well end up in an entirely different mindset from where they started—and that will affect their final choice, often to their own surprise. The process is so far from linear that it is in fact quite messy. The touchpoints for engaging consumers do not run from A to B in a straight line, but are spread erratically all across the customer journey.

To navigate this contemporary version of the purchase funnel, the Super Strategist needs to reimagine how people get exposed to and consume brands at any given point, to understand not only "what makes them tick," but also how their attitudes and behaviors change continuously, as they move along the path to purchase. Modern strategic planning needs to lead the charge in customer journey mapping. By pulling in all relevant disciplines (often including external agency partners, such as PR or other specialized firms), using proprietary research, and leading journey workshops, planners can recreate that meandering path to better understand the events leading up to the final decision: where the consumer enters, leaves, and reenters the process; how they make decisions, using their heart or head, throughout the process; and, importantly, how they feel about the whole experience, and how they share the outcome. (For more on customer journeys—the most important tool in any account planner's tool kit—see Chapter 8.)

Today, brand touchpoints and experiences are not siloed—they are spread across your entire customer journey

Push Notifcation

TV/Video/Outdoor

Lead Gen

White Paper Download

Dynamic Digital

The modern customer journey is complex, with many brand touchpoints spread haphazardly along the way, creating challenges for strategic planners.

Brand Stewardship

For brand leaders, the advertising agency plays a vital role. Agencies generate the big brand and creative ideas and serve as the aggregators, curators, and stewards of the brand, the consumer, and all the brand experiences that constitute the customer journey—which the agency, with its multichannel approach and consumer expertise, should own. Strategic planners within an agency help CMOs make brand choices based on strategic direction, versus simply on what's shiny and new.

Sometimes our clients' understanding of ad agencies and what "advertising" should do for them is as conflicted as our own, and many CMOs are seeing their budgets shrink or be cannibalized by other divisions within their organizations. As they desperately chase consumers to the next digital platform, CMOs are asking themselves if the agency of record (AOR) model (wherein a single agency executes a comprehensive brand approach) is the best way to win customers in today's frenzied marketplace. Seeking best in class, many clients prefer to work with multiple agencies representing different marketing specialties.

This approach has its merits, but an AOR is best qualified to put the pieces together into one brand story. Why is this still important? Well, if the CMO wants to retain brand integrity, and protect and nurture their brand, then they—and the strategic planners at their agency—need to become the brand's steward. If the brand is not well defined, brand anarchy is inevitable: each specialist agency partner and every brand stakeholder could redefine the brand in any way they like, based on whatever they believe about the brand at any given moment. This will never be consistent and will create confusion for the consumer—who, remember, seeks consistency in brands.

The brand stewards on the client and agency side have to firmly define the brand purpose, vision, positioning, personality, and brand identity (typically, these take the form of one unified brand house) and filter all brand decisions through this definition. Decisions that include sponsorships, affiliations, partnerships, packaging, new product development (NPD), websites, in-store experiences, uniforms, business cards, annual reports—every single potential experience of the brand, internal and external.

While "best-in-class" specialist agencies can be incredibly valuable to the CMO, they are only involved in part of the brand experience. And while brand consulting firms are well qualified for this kind of work, they are expensive, their timelines are typically longer, and their job is complete when the brand assets have been created, and so they then move on to the next project.

Because the AOR team is constantly involved in the whole brand picture, and because they use the brand assets in the day-to-day work that they do for their clients, I believe they are best positioned to know if these assets are not just solid in principle, but also that they will actually function properly as a guide and inspiration to the development of strategies and then creative ideas and channel plans for their clients.

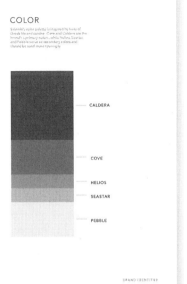

COLOR

Saloniki's color palette is inspired by hues of Greek life and cuisine. Cove and Caldera are the brand's primary colors, while Helios, Seastar and Pebble serve as secondary colors and should be used more sparingly.

.... CALDERA

.... COVE

.... HELIOS

.... SEASTAR

.... PEBBLE

BRAND IDENTITY9

The visual identity guidelines for Saloniki Greek, a restaurant group in Boston, include a color palette "inspired by hues of Greek life and cuisine." Created by Karen Hite of Hill Holliday, 2018.

It is therefore the strategic planner at the AOR who will often partner with clients (especially those who do not have the budgets or appetite for brand consulting firms) to define and secure the different assets of the brand. These, ideally, become solidified through the production of a brand book that features visual identity guidelines and the brand house (see the next chapter). Consumers today are confused and overwhelmed by too much choice. They rely on brands to help them make decisions, and to do that they need a consistent brand experience. The brand book becomes the blueprint that all partners and stakeholders adhere to. But before you can create that plan for the future, you need to know where you are right now.

Which Brand Family Are You In?

You may recall my earlier reference to the basic elements of the planning cycle (see page 9), as identified by Stephen King of JWT. The key questions are:

1. Where are we?
2. Why are we there?
3. Where could we be?
4. How could we get there?
5. Are we getting there?

These questions are still meaningful today. The brand family is a great tool to help the strategic planner answer the first three. I believe that brands fall into four general groups: Alpha, Youth, Old Dog, and Newborn.

ALPHA

These are the established leaders and power players in their category. Alpha brands are typically the first brand consumers, if asked, will recall unaided and with incredibly positive brand sentiment. A decade and more ago, Alpha brands were fast-food brands or consumer goods, such as McDonald's, Nike, Coke, and Tide. Today's Alpha brands include e-commerce and technology brands, such as Amazon, Apple, and Google.

For Alpha brands to hold their brand dominance and leadership, they have to:

- stay relevant to changing consumer attitudes and behaviors by constantly tracking cultural, consumer, and competitive trends. For example, to instantly predict what products may appeal to individual customers, Amazon's AI tracks consumer behavior informed by the long-standing consumer trends of time starvation and the continued need for instant gratification.

- continue to appeal to new target audiences. A perfect example of this is the Old Spice campaign that I mentioned earlier: the work was so provocative that they ran the risk of losing their existing older male

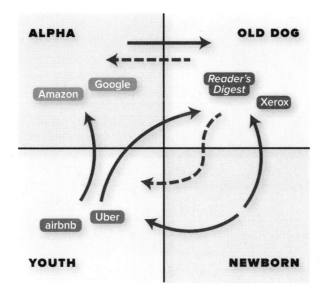

Examples of where some of today's most famous brands fall in the brand family chart. Solid arrows indicate possible transitions, desirable or not. Dashed arrows indicate unlikely transitions unless radical action is taken.

consumers, but that was outweighed by the risk of not evolving to appeal to younger men.

- continue to invest in relevant advertising and communications that affirm brand leadership

If Alpha brands do not do these things, they may lose their leadership status or, much worse, slip into the Old Dog category. Think of a traditional car brand like Cadillac, which has struggled to stay relevant to younger consumers, who now associate the brand with their grandparents' pursuit of the American Dream.

YOUTH

These are fledgling brands, 20 years old or younger, typically challengers that broke into a category with an unconventional and better consumer offering (think Airbnb and JetBlue). Often, these brands build a business and a brand at the same time, but on occasion, they build the business and forgo the brand. In that case, by the time they are in their late childhood/early teen years, and investors are demanding new growth, a brand needs to be quickly established, then they invite agencies to pitch. Youth brands will typically stay in a very strong position if they:

- stay ahead of the curve by staying extremely close to cultural shifts, forcing competitors to recalibrate to them

- keep their current audiences engaged, while continuously building connections with new audiences

- retain a challenger mindset, instead of slipping into conventional behaviors

If Youth brands do these things, they will either retain their current position or grow to become Alpha brands. An example of this would be Airbnb, which tapped into two cultural shifts: the first being the slow breakdown of community, and the subsequent need for people to feel a sense of belonging elsewhere; the second being the consumers' desire to enjoy a fully immersive cultural experience when traveling, rather than staying in a generic hotel. If brands do not work to retain relevance, there's a danger of slipping directly into Old Dog oblivion. Think Blockbuster, which ignored the shift to streaming video and swiftly collapsed.

OLD DOG

Alpha brands that fail to continually invest in maintaining brand relevancy will turn into Old Dogs. Think *Reader's Digest*, once the best-selling magazine in the U.S., now associated with medical waiting rooms. It is very hard to teach an Old Dog new tricks and revitalize the brand, but it is possible, if the brand team:

- recognizes that complete reinvention is necessary for survival

- relaunches itself in a way that is new, relevant, but also authentic through exciting new product launches and fresh new advertising campaigns

· realizes that the only way forward is to focus on new audiences, rather than trying to reinvigorate old audiences who have died off or moved away from the brand—agencies are constantly being asked by clients of Old Dog brands to appeal to new audiences without alienating existing ones. The bigger risk is focusing on existing audiences and continuing to alienate new ones.

If there is a type of brand that needs to take risks, this is it. Better to be remembered as the CMO who tried radical new things and succeeded or even failed, than the CMO who killed a decades-old brand on their watch, by doing nothing of any significance.

For a superb (but rare) example of how to beautifully resurrect an Old Dog, check out the Tango Orange campaign created by my last UK agency, London's Howell Henry Chaldecott Lury (HHCL). Sales were so poor the brand was close to being taken off grocery shelves. As legend has it, the client came to the agency with £1 million and essentially gave the team strategic and creative license. The agency and client brand teams developed a now-famous TV campaign, targeting British teens, that was the antithesis of American soda commercials of the time (think big hair and big music). The first ad featured a round orange-painted man who slapped the sides of a blue-collar Englishman's head when he sipped a can of Tango Orange, and ended with the tagline, "You'll know when you've been Tango'd." Despite the tiny spend, the campaign gained so much attention that it propelled the brand from near death to the number three slot, right behind Coke and Pepsi, in 1 year. It also won numerous awards and helped HHCL be named "Agency of the Decade" by *Campaign* magazine in 1990.

A brave client and a brave agency did something that was almost impossible—but it required a radical new way of thinking and an unbelievably bold, groundbreaking, and risky campaign idea.

NEWBORN

As the name implies, these brands are completely new, with no consumer awareness or consideration. But they can easily move straight to Old Dog status. Consider Vonage or Garmin GPS, which both hit the scene with a flurry of attention, but failed to jump ahead of the curve and evolve their technology to match fast-changing consumer needs. In order for Newborns to move into Youth brand status, they need to:

- invest in product development and advertising to increase awareness and consideration

- push against category conventions to offer a clearly superior service or product

- be a challenger in all brand communications. Newborns get no attention if their brand launch is conventional; unless it surprises them into paying attention, consumers will misattribute boring advertising to a better-known brand, which will, in turn, thank you for your free investment.

Using the brand family tool, client and agency teams can plot a brand's current status through sales data and consumer research, though most will have a good sense of where their brand sits, and then identify what needs to be done to help it survive and/or thrive. From there, a strategic plan can be developed, and one of the primary tools to help a brand create a vision for reinvention, or even survival, is the brand house.

four

The Brand House

OCCASIONALLY, A TRIED-AND-TRUE planning tool endures through radical changes in the industry because it is almost impossible to improve upon. Modern strategic planning has no use for the purchase funnel, but a tool of a similar vintage, the brand house, is so incredibly useful it may be of value forever.

The brand house consolidates all brand assets into one chart, which makes things easier. With a strong brand house, decision-making within the brand is easier, telling the story of the brand clearly and consistently is easier, and for the consumer, understanding the brand and its values is easier. If it all aligns, consumers become predisposed to the brand before they are ready to make a choice. The brand house, particularly the purpose and pillars, also has a profound effect on the beliefs and behaviors of a company's internal audience—its employees.

I have worked with brands that have transformed their business by developing and sticking to their brand house. From 2015-19, I consulted with Calvin Klein, which was in a tough situation in the mid-2010s. As everyone knows, the fashion brand achieved global fame in the 1980s, but more recently it had become mostly a main-stream department store brand. Beautiful collection dresses appeared at red carpets on celebrities like Kendall Jenner, Jennifer Lawrence, and Lupita Nyong'o—but the brand could also be found at Costco for a few dollars for a pack of underwear. Global sales were flat or declining.

In my very first assignment, I was commissioned to do global consumer research. It told us that young consumers from Asia to Europe to Latin America all felt that the brand was living off the vapors of its past fame (if you are above a certain age, you may remember the famous Brooke Shields and Kate Moss ads), and it was universally felt that within a year or so younger Millennials and emerging Gen Zers would lose interest completely. The brand was sliding towards irrelevance and oblivion.

Despite having significant sales globally, Calvin Klein was a classic Alpha brand that was quickly on its way to becoming an Old Dog. The culprit, as usual, was neglect: a lack of real investment in advertising for many years, meaning a lack of relevant and modern brand messaging and, critically, the lack of a brand house. Without a "North Star" to guide the brand, each region had "gone rogue" and produced campaigns that were not consistent with the master brand, or did nothing to define the future of the brand. Total brand anarchy.

In collaboration with another consultant, we developed the brand house in two workshops, then the brave and talented marketing and creative team championed it and rolled it out globally. First, though, we implemented the brand house across the internal Calvin Klein brand experience, from recruitment to training. The *brand positioning*, in particular, would influence not only the creative, but also every choice that the brand would subsequently make, from hiring, to design, and even to the transformation of their new office space. A brand positioning statement (see "Brand Positioning," page 51, in this chapter) describes how a product or service fills a consumer need. The words we landed on were:

Calvin Klein. Modern Provocateur.

The positioning captured the essence of the brand's beginning, when Calvin Klein himself had been the epitome of the "modern provocateur," as well as the later Kate Moss campaign. Ultimately, it reminded the team of the heritage of the brand: they were sitting on the shoulders of giants, which should give them a sense of pride, not terror.

To be relevant to a teen to early 30s audience, they had to poke the bear. They had to redefine what being "modern" and "provocative" meant for the brand. Because what it meant in the 1990s was totally irrelevant to Millennial and older Gen Z audiences, who had been born digital and social natives and were, to date, fairly unshockable. Today, relevance is being transparent and authentic. In advertising, Gen Zers and younger Millennials expect celebrities to be genuine and true. They don't just want to see images of pretty faces. They want to understand the person, to hear the backstory—the hard knocks, as well as the highs. They also want diversity. Different ethnicities, different age groups, different abilities, different bodies, and different sexual orientations.

Inspired by the brand positioning, the creative director created a radical new advertising campaign that was initially launched featuring Justin Bieber. Bieber was at an important crossroads; he had started making great music again after a period of self-destructive behavior had taken the sheen off his glittering career. The marketing and creative team, led by Melisa Goldie, Bob Fouhy, Lina Kutsovskaya, and Michael DeLellis, took a chance on hiring him. If this worked, it would resurrect not only his career, but also the Calvin Klein brand. Or the exact opposite could have happened. Much to their credit, the team decided to go for it.

The subsequent #MYCALVINS campaign was the shot in the arm the brand needed to revive itself. People were intrigued to see Justin Bieber looking so fantastic and were keen to learn more about where he was in his life and career. The campaign launch was almost 100 percent paid social, and social mentions for Calvin Klein rapidly spiked over the period when the ads ran and stayed high for a number of weeks afterwards. The campaign was extended over the next 12 months and other diverse celebrities signed up to show the world what they, too, did in their Calvins. The campaign has evolved and is still running strong as this goes to press.

The campaign that began the transformation of Calvin Klein's flattening business was inspired by the brand house we built. It's the blueprint informing all brand decisions—business cards, billion-dollar global campaigns, and everything in between. When the entire leadership team buys into the brand house, and encourages their employees to live it every day, transformation is possible.

The brand house is foundational to a brand, but that doesn't mean it needs to be set in stone. It will evolve to reflect changes in the company, culture, category, and, of course, the economy. But ideally, the brand house should stand unscathed for a few years, at least. So, it's important to get the elements right. But first, you need to know what a brand house looks like.

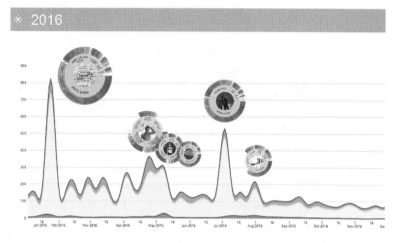

Calvin Klein's #MYCALVINS campaign, featuring Justin Bieber, caused a spike in social media mentions—the KPI that matters in fashion, where brand relevance is everything.

The Architecture of a Brand House

There are many variants of brand houses, and you need to find the one that works best for you. The structure that I use is shown on the facing page. Whatever model you choose, each part of the brand house plays a distinct role. As with a real house, if one part is removed, destroyed, or neglected, the structure will weaken or collapse. The brand house can be improved upon over time (just as a house can be refurbished), but for the brand to remain whole, everyone who touches the brand, now and in the future, must respect and adhere to it.

The tried, tested, and true brand house—a timeless tool for any strategic planner.

BRAND PURPOSE

There is much talk today about "purpose-driven brands," as social media has forced brands to be transparent and authentic. Ultimately, that is a good thing: social media has moved power from the brand to the consumer, who will only engage with or buy from brands that share their values. A brand's most critical value should be reflected in the brand purpose—this is the roof of the house and its most important element. In a brand house workshop, you always start at the top, as it will influence every other element in a positive and inspiring way.

This is the purpose of the brand beyond profit, the reason why the company and brand even exist. It answers the questions: What do we stand for as a company? What impact do we want to make on the world? The brand purpose often gets confused with the brand mission, and a simple way to distinguish them is to think of the mission as "*what* we do" and the purpose as "*why* we do it." It is the most humanized aspect of the brand house and of the company's unified vision. It is owned by everyone, but it is typically championed by the CEO and/or chairperson.

A brand purpose must:

· be true to who the brand is now

· inspire the whole company

· instill a sense of pride

· lay the foundation for future improvement

· be ongoing and unreachable; that is, it may be so aspirational that it is impossible to achieve, but the brand will never stop trying

· be simple and use natural, consumer language

Following are some examples of brand purpose statements that can be found online. (Note that some of these brands identify these statements as mission or vision statements. The terminology has become confused over the years, but I would suggest that these are indeed purpose statements.)

Dove: To help women everywhere develop a positive relationship with the way they look, helping them realize their full potential.

Crayola: Encouraging children to be creative and enabling parents to inspire them.

Disney: To create happiness for others.

Note that the simpler the purpose, the more likely employees and stakeholders are to remember it.

The brand purpose typically pushes against a *cultural nemesis.* In the case of Disney, I can imagine discussions about how people are becoming more anxious and depressed, as the pressures of work and life build up with each passing year. This isn't an idle generalization, but an insight based on solid data: according to a recent American Psychiatric Association poll, almost 40 percent of Americans were more anxious in 2019 than the year before. With a nemesis identified, brand managers can then ask how their brand could become the antidote. If people are anxious or sad, the antidote could be "happiness." If the world is complex, the antidote could be "simplicity."

To illustrate how to get to a brand purpose in a brand house workshop, let's return to Sally's, our imaginary brand of mac and cheese. Let's say that it's a family-owned business that has been around for 40 years, with strong family values. Sally's is proud to use a few simple, natural ingredients, with no colorings or additives.

First, ask the team why the brand exists at all. Then, to find your cultural nemesis, examine and discuss the key dynamics that are animating the culture at large today. For example, in the U.S. we have never been more divided as a country. So, if you are pushing against "division," then the antidote could be "togetherness." Or, "inequality" gets you to "inclusion." "Hate" or "cynicism" is combatted with "love."

Let's find a succinct way of putting this all together. For Sally's, our purpose statement could be: "We bring love to any table."

Now you have the top of the house.

A brand's purpose statement speaks to why a brand exists, beyond profit motives.

BRAND MISSION

Some brand houses refer to the brand mission, while others use the term brand vision. To me, they are almost interchangeable. However, since a vision typically focuses on a future state that is often not achievable in anyone on the brand team's lifetime, and since the brand purpose already does this to some extent, I like the next level of the brand house to be more achievable and tangible.

The brand mission is a short narrative that outlines what the company does, or intends to do. It is true to who the brand is now and leaves some wiggle room for the future. It is related to the brand purpose, but is more descriptive and uses more concrete language. The mission is owned by the whole company, but is typically championed by the CFO and COO.

The brand mission needs to:

- be informed by the brand's unique or superior product benefits
- focus on what the brand needs to do now and in the future to make an impact
- be achievable within the lifetime of the company
- be short, succinct, and rational

Examples of brand missions that can be found online are:

Amazon.com: To be the earth's most customer-centric company.

Microsoft: To empower every person and every organization on the planet to achieve more.

Tesla: To accelerate the world's transition to sustainable energy.

Now, using these guidelines, let's create a brand mission for Sally's Mac and Cheese. First, the brand's superior benefits are twofold: it is family-owned, and the ingredients are natural and of a high quality. Because of this, the brand charges a premium over the competition. Next, we need to identify how the brand makes or could make an impact on people's lives. Sally's brings families together around the dinner table, as the meal is typically presented in a serving dish that is to be shared. There is another important piece of information to consider: the longer-term objective of the brand is to create new products beyond mac and cheese, such as cottage pie and sweet potato casserole. These new products will remain in the higher-end comfort food category, because this is Sally's point of difference. So, we need to have a mission that is relevant for now *and* for later, such as: "To create superior shareable food that brings families together."

We bring love
to any table

To create superior shareable food
that brings families together

The brand mission identifies an achievable goal for the company.

BRAND POSITIONING

The brand positioning is often confused with a value proposition, another term often used in marketing. However, these terms are somewhat different. A value proposition tends to be broader and describes how the product or service is superior to the competition, or the benefit it provides the consumer. Positioning statements speak to how the benefits of the product or service fill a consumer need. The brand positioning is the space and place the brand occupies in the consumer's mind.

Unlike the brand purpose or mission statement, a positioning statement is not intended to be public facing. It is typically short, memorable, and the most critical phrase in a creative brief, under the "single proposition" section. The brand positioning is typically championed by marketing and communications.

The brand positioning needs to:

- be brief and clear
- be unique and memorable
- be differentiated
- be true to your brand and your values
- define the brand benefit that is delivered to consumers

Examples of brand positionings I have found online are:

Dollar Shave Club: A great shave, cheap.

Uber: The smartest way to get around.

Slack: Be more productive at work with less effort.

HubSpot: There's a better way to grow.

Sally's Mac and Cheese has many differentiated brand benefits versus the competition. It is nutritious and chemical-free, whereas the main competitor uses food coloring and synthetic flavoring and is high in carbs and salt. Sally's is made from high-quality ingredients, making it more expensive, whereas the main competitor is cheaper but uses cheap ingredients. All brands of mac and cheese are comfort food loved by families; they are often among a small repertoire of foods that kids will actually eat. But parents may worry about these foods being unhealthy. So how about releasing them from guilt by offering "comfort food that's actually good for you."

The brand positioning (bottom) is the most important element of a creative brief. It should be short and memorable.

BRAND PILLARS

The pillars are the hardworking structures that make the house solid. Without them it will crumble. Brand pillars take on different forms depending on a brand's needs, but I ask clients to strictly adhere to only three pillars, for three reasons: it requires discipline to pare down to three pillars; three pillars are easier to remember; and three pillars are easier to execute.

The last point is particularly important because often the brand pillars are directives for the employees who are "boots on the ground"—they will be lived by consumer-facing employees and are thus the most prominent. With Dunkin' Donuts, one of our former clients, we all agreed that Dunkin' needed pillars that acted as simple directives to the servers, who typically worked at Dunkin' for a short time before churning out. The pillars couldn't be ethereal or broad. The pillars needed to support the upper elements of the house, and for Dunkin' this was not possible without getting the basics of customer service and quality control right. One example of this was "get it right the first time."

For other service brands, the pillars could be individual words that reflect what the service experience needs to be. For an Old Dog brand, pillar words like "innovative" or "progressive" are important to bring energy and dynamism to the brand. *However*, do *not* use these words if your brand has no intention of innovating or being progressive. It sounds really obvious, but very often, clients will want to overextend the pillar language into promises that for a variety of reasons, such as budget, manufacturing, or distribution, they cannot keep. Broken pillars (and, therefore, broken promises), render the brand house useless. Stick with pillars that:

- reflect what the brand is now, with some wiggle room

- offer useful, practical direction or an attainable vision for the brand

- are simple and easy to understand and communicate

- define what the brand must *do* to live the brand purpose, mission, and positioning

Examples of brand pillars I have found online:

Southwest: Warrior Spirit/Servant's Heart/Fun-Loving Attitude

John Deere: Quality/Integrity/Innovation

It is important to understand the customers' experience of the brand before you start pillar development. Ask your team: How is the service, online and in-store? Are the basics covered, or is there a lot of work to do? How about the product quality? Is it consistent? Is the company seen as an innovator or a laggard? Can the company innovate quickly? The responses to these questions will inform the types of pillars you need to create—whether they offer practical guidance or an attainable vision. You may even need a combination of both.

For Sally's Mac and Cheese, let's look at the imperatives for the family and the brand:

· Sally's creates a superior product, but there have been some complaints of a lack of quality consistency over the last 11 months, with many returns of late.

· The company has manufactured the same three varieties of mac and cheese for 10 years and is considered by consumers to be more sluggish than competitive brands, but there is a solid plan to develop at least two new types of quality comfort food products within the next 12–18 months.

· Sally's factory workers and ground staff have developed a strong sense of community and kinship, which isn't experienced in other departments, such as marketing, PR, or sales. The owners understand the importance of family and community, and want to ensure that their values are expanded into and lived by the whole organization, not just the factory workers, since they are a family and their products are consumed by families.

These imperatives suggest that to support the brand house, Sally's pillars need to combine guidance and vision, such as:

1. consistent quality
2. dynamic innovation
3. strong family values

Brand pillars are the RTBS (reasons to believe) that support the rest of the brand house. Without these, the whole structure would crumble.

BRAND PERSONALITY

The brand personality is the foundation of the brand house, supporting the entire structure. It is the most human of the brand house elements. It needs to describe the brand as if it were a person, in a way the consumer can relate to. The brand personality is owned by the entire company.

To establish a successful brand personality, ask yourself:

· Would the "person" be male or female?
· How would you best describe that "person"?
· What makes this "person" likeable and interesting?

At best, the brand personality needs to:

· be three words, maximum

- use descriptors that can coexist (instead of being opposites or clashing)
- use the most consumer-friendly language in the house
- reflect the past, present, and future of the brand

Examples of brand personalities found online:

Etsy: Honest. Unique. Hardworking.

Beats by Dr. Dre: Young. Trendy. Rugged.

Harley-Davidson: Macho. Adventurous. Free.

For Sally's Mac and Cheese, the personality of the brand represents the personality of the members of the family who founded it. Like the family, the brand is as real as can be, trustworthy to a fault, and generous to others, so, for our brand personality, how about:

Authentic. Honest. Kind.

The foundation of a brand house is the personality—if the brand were a person, how would its friends describe it? The completed brand house informs all decisions made by everyone who touches the brand.

Now we've completed the Sally's Mac and Cheese brand house. If Sally's were a real company, this would be the blueprint for all brand decision-making. Sally's would have a purpose and vision to work towards, one known by every partner, vendor, agency, and stakeholder. It would create clarity, simplicity, and discipline around the brand, leaving no room for either personal interpretation or brand anarchy. It would influence the visual identity of the brand, the types of product they produced, the advertising they created, and the kinds of employees they would hire, from the factory floors to the C-Suite. Its pillars would inform the boots on the ground, giving them values and practices to adhere to.

Frequently, regardless of how successful a brand is, when a new CMO is hired the brand is reinvented, and valuable brand assets are thrown away, sometimes simply because they "weren't invented here." A strong brand house will outlive most employees and prevent this needless reinvention. The house becomes bigger than the brand team who created it and any that follow them.

Building a Brand House

You will be surprised at how many brands out there do not have a brand house or anything like it. It's amazing to me how anyone gets anything done without it, considering how much time must be wasted in trying to redefine the brand over and over, instead of sticking to one blueprint. If the marketing team you are working with does not have a brand house (or something similar), try to convince them of its importance, and then set up a full-day or 2-day workshop as soon as possible.

ATTENDEES

This workshop should be run by the strategic planners on the business, and there should be no more than about 20 people present. Participants should consist of:

- key agency team members from core departments, including creative, account management, connections/media planning, content design, user experience (UX), and social/digital strategy (our strategists are integrated but if yours are not, invite each). Make sure your agency team is of a manageable size: 6–8 people is ideal.

· key relevant specialist partner agency team members (maximum of 4 people). Now, I know that working with partner agencies can sometimes be a strain for all concerned, but when it comes to brand house development, getting different brains into the room, with different perspectives, and who have a stake in the outcome, is very important.

· key day-to-day clients: if possible, the CEO or president of the company, and others who can provide important input, such as HR, sales, merchandising, etc. Let your client guide you on this. Again, 6–8 people, tops.

THE FLOW OF THE WORKSHOP

The structure of the workshop can be adapted depending on your client's needs and availability. But in general, below I have outlined what has worked for me over the last few years:

1. explain the objectives of the workshop and the rules of engagement:

   a. leave your title at the door
   b. leave your phone by the door, turned off (good luck with that)
   c. think more like a consumer (or customer if the brand is B2B)
   d. keep it simple
   e. most of each "layer" of the final brand house should be easily remembered by anyone with a few minutes of exposure to it. (I sometimes flash a favorite brand house in front of them for two minutes, then take it away and ask them what they remember. This usually does the trick.)

2. explain each element of the brand house in detail and offer notes

3. show examples of each element and offer notes

4. show examples of complete brand houses (with the usual proprietary caveats)

5. give each person a pile of blank brand house worksheets

6. ask each individual to create two brand houses quickly: one that flows naturally from them (to encourage them to note assets that they think are important to the brand now), and one that scares them a little (to force them to think differently about what the brand could be)

7. be sure to have a pad and easel in the room to note down anything important that the team does not truly understand or know well enough in order to be able to complete the brand house with confidence. These notes will help identify knowledge gaps that may require some further digging or the commissioning of new consumer research.

8. split the group into three teams

9. ask each group to discuss each person's two brand houses, then create two team brand houses—same approach as before

10. ask each team to present their two brand houses to the group

11. work together as one whole team to try to create one brand house that is true to the brand as it is today, but that leaves wiggle room and ambition for the future. You will most likely end up with two or three different flavors of brand houses. The most important thing to avoid is a compromised brand house that checks boxes and keeps everyone happy, but that inspires no one. Regularly encourage everyone to be bold and to keep it simple.

12. by the end of the workshop, you should have some draft brand houses that you and your agency team can work with to create the optimal master brand house that you can refine with your clients and agree upon after a few rounds of discussion over the next week or two

13. design the brand house beautifully. The better and more professional it looks, the less likely it is to be picked apart (honestly, this is true).

THE BRAND HOUSE IS NOT JUST A MARKETING TOOL

Now, this next part is incredibly important. After you've built the brand house, the work is just beginning. You must engage client groups in the adoption of the brand house, or it will become just another chart that marketing created, languishing in some long-forgotten file at the back of everyone's desk drawer.

First, engage the CEO. The best way to get buy-in is to pull them in when the brand house is in draft form. Let the CEO focus on the brand purpose and brand mission. They are more likely to want to own, and regularly repeat, the purpose in their town hall meetings, investor meetings, thought leadership papers, panels and speeches, and, of course, annual reports. After all, the brand purpose is the North Star of the whole organization. Its reason for being. It makes sense for the leader to own it. Plus, the rest of the C-Suite will buy into the brand house if the CEO has already approved it, and if employees hear them use it regularly, then they'll do the same.

If the CEO creates a different brand purpose that you like just as much as the one you developed, and it fits with the rest of the brand house, use it. If they tweak yours and it doesn't kill the essence of it, use it. The CEO will be the brand purpose's biggest champion.

Next, you need to engage the employees. It's one thing to remember the elements of the brand house, it's another to actually adopt and *live* them every day. There is only one guaranteed way to ensure this: have your clients set up mini-workshops, starting with critical teams such as HR and sales. Have each department run their workshop by focusing on the following agenda:

- discussion about the brand house—how the company and their department currently live or do not live it

- discussion about how their department needs to evolve or adapt to live the brand house day to day

- agreement on actions that will be taken to ensure that their department lives, eats, sleeps, and breathes the brand house

After the workshops, each department can present their plan to the C-Suite—including the CMO—and make a clear commitment to executing it, within an agreed-upon time period, with support from the C-Suite, as needed.

By being actively involved and gaining some ownership, each department will be more likely to buy in to the brand house and implement the changes, which will change behaviors within their team. As each team adapts, the overall company starts to move towards the purpose and mission outlined in the brand house. Instead of being an intangible and, therefore, dismissible document, it becomes a real living blueprint.

five

Modern Consumer Research

AGENCIES FREQUENTLY DO their best work during the pitch process. That is because at this early stage, the pitch team typically knows very little about the brand. They are thinking objectively, more like consumers, and developing work that is intuitive.

A key role of account management is to develop strong client relationships. The modern account management team must understand the client's business almost as well as the clients do, so they can continually steer the agency team towards the client's goals—not just brand success, but also positive *business* outcomes. As the account team learns the category dynamics, it is almost impossible for them to continue to be objective.

The most important role of strategic planners is to represent the consumer (or customer) throughout the process of developing communications. They can only do so by remaining unbiased. Modern strategic planners should have strong client relationships and a firm grasp of the client's business goals, but to maintain objectivity they typically do not spend as much time with clients as their account management partners do. To pull the voice of the consumer into strategy and advertising development as much as possible, strategic planners have always used research as a primary tool. Whether it's working with a client's research department or personally conducting or commissioning research on behalf of the client, consumer research offers a vital glimpse into the mind of the ultimate judge of a campaign's efficacy.

There are literally hundreds of research methodologies out there. To name just a few: in-store mobile ethnographies, consumer neuroscience research, biometric market research (measuring a respondents physical response to stimuli using, for example, heart rate monitoring), predictive modeling, virtual shopping (virtual store simulation), user experience research (online and in-store), conjoint analysis (surveys that test different market attributes, from location, audience, and product to find which combination is most effective or influential), segmentation studies (that help you determine your best audience segments), and tracking studies (tracking brand or ad health over time).

In addition, there is a slew of newer tools available through brands like Google Analytics that help optimize campaigns and website experiences, including:

- the number of users on a website

- traffic and usage changes on a website after a campaign launch

- the effects of social sharing

- the location of different audiences and their interests

- the devices and channels that audiences favor

- the tracking of marketing campaigns

- conversion rates and top-selling products

Whether it's qualitative, for example, focus groups or individual ethnographies, or quantitative, which typically means surveys conducted online, research is most useful when it is aimed at gathering information, not evaluating creative ideas.

Testing the Creative(s)

Decades ago, research meant one thing—focus groups: a group of eight or so people gathered in a focus group facility (or in the case of the UK, in a hostess's living room) in a discussion led by a moderator or the planner, with agency people observing through a one-way mirror. Focus groups can be a great way to gather information about consumers and gain insight into their relationship with your category and brand.

But there is a reason why creatives call focus groups "f*ck-us groups." When focus groups are used to test creative ideas, this type of research will often kill great work. Why? Any experienced ad person knows that great work is supposed to defy category convention, stand out, and, ultimately, claim a unique, primary position in the consumer's brain.

If you ask a group of regular consumers to judge creative ideas— especially those in conceptual stage—most will question why an idea does not follow convention. They will kill an idea that "does not compute" or suggest changes to make the idea easier for them to understand. This makes the work generic—which sells categories, not brands.

If I asked you to create a plausible casual dining ad, you would know exactly what to do. Start with smiling wait staff, delivering trays of piping-hot food to delighted families. Add close-ups of melting butter on thick steaks, manicured hands squeezing lemon over salmon fillets and pulling apart crusty, steaming breadsticks. Essentially, what we call "food porn." You get it.

This is the type of generic ad that is borne from a vicious cycle: an ad agency presents a bold creative idea. The client is anxious that this idea is "too creative" and persuades the agency to include more conventional work in the testing. Both the bold and conventional ideas are tested in focus groups. Respondents reject the bold work and choose the creative that fits with what they have already seen multiple times. To them, that is what a casual dining ad should look like. Anything that breaks the mold is not their idea of appealing advertising. At best, generic work like this falls into the realm of "do no harm." At worst, it is boring and easily misattributed. What is certain is that it is never good, and it rarely works.

What it boils down to is this consumer sentiment:

> I think I like it . . .
> But I fear it.
> Therefore, I reject it.

Remember the Tango ad that I mentioned in an earlier chapter? As I recollect the order of events, the team was asked to test the TV concept, and the young adult respondents rejected it in the first round of research. But the team believed that this ad was special and went for it anyway, targeting an even younger audience and succeeding beyond belief. Great concepts make you feel excited and terrified all at the same time. That's what groundbreaking creative ideas do. And that's how good advertising works.

Advertising works on an unconscious as well as a conscious level, especially TV/video advertising. And consumers will only view ads if they are engaging and entertaining. Remember Apple's iconic "1984" ad? The spot is considered a masterpiece, among the most effective of the 20th century. In it, a female runner pursued by men in riot gear enters an auditorium full of blank-eyed drones and throws a hammer at the huge screen they're watching, smashing it to pieces. On the surface, the ad is a brief and cryptic vignette followed by an Apple logo. Subconsciously, it is saying that if you are someone who likes to believe you are different than other people, if you are someone who likes to break the rules, if you seek superior brands that defy convention and raise the bar—then Apple is for you.

The consumer unconsciously understands this. When they are in the market to buy a computer, they will be predisposed towards

Apple, but may not remember why. They will cite rational reasons for the purchase, such as "it was a good price" or "I loved the design." But the real reasons for purchasing that particular brand are much more complicated, and not easily defined by consumers. Ads are supposed to make you feel something and/or do something. But you don't really need to understand it or be able to explain it, because it is not a logical, left-brain process. That is what makes it so hard to test creative in qualitative research.

There are rare exceptions, though. One type of focus group can actually *protect* good work, and that is hypnosis focus groups, where the unconscious mind does most of the work. I observed hypnosis focus groups reveal the importance of branding in the telecoms category. Consciously, respondents told us that design and branding did not matter to them in the slightest. However, when put into a light hypnotic trance (yes, they all signed waivers), respondents told us that design was very important to them. In this instance, the bright colors and contemporary design of the Cingular logo (they had just been bought out and were about to endure a major AT&T rebrand) made them feel that the brand was modern and more European than other American brands, like Verizon and AT&T. To them, the design made Cingular feel young and upscale, and, therefore, more appealing.

I am not suggesting that you do hypnosis focus groups every time you want to test branding design or creative ideas; I am just trying to prove a point here. Consumers are simply not very good at judging groundbreaking creative.

If your client absolutely insists on it, or if you are testing the work for your team as a disaster check, before presenting to a client or for a pitch, test the work monadically (one concept per cell of consumers) in a quantitative online survey. You will need to expose each idea to at least five hundred-plus consumers for the results to be anywhere near more than directional.

It may not match the traditional definition of a focus group, but this sort of quantitative research gives you the ability to craft only relevant and useful questions and exclude those that force the consumer to consciously judge the work. For example, instead of "Do you like this idea?" you may ask, "Is the idea different from other ideas you have seen in this category?" or "Is this idea memorable?" It doesn't matter if a consumer "likes" an idea or not. As long as it is not offensive to them, what's important is that they *remember* the idea, see it as being different, talk about it with their family and friends, and act on it when the time comes for them to do so.

The only other type of basic concept testing that I would recommend is AB testing. AB testing (powered by platforms like Google Analytics) is a great way to test and optimize content in market, in real time. Assuming all other variants (ad design, spend, size, audience, etc.) are more or less equal, different digital ads are launched into the world, each with the same media weight behind them. The effectiveness of each is determined by the number of clicks each gets. As this is tracked, in real time, media spend is redirected to support the most successful messages, with the highest clicks or conversion rates, while the less effective messages are either changed or pulled.

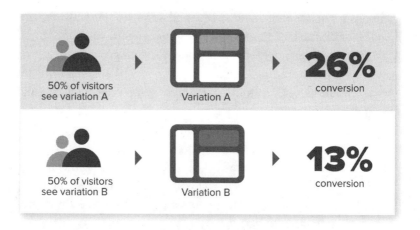

50% of visitors see variation A — Variation A — **26%** conversion

50% of visitors see variation B — Variation B — **13%** conversion

If you must test creative, AB testing is one of the most effective means.

Sadly, some clients are often overdependent on creative testing. They use research as a means of trying to validate that ads will "work" when in market. They then become incapable of making a decision because they have become too dependent on the consumer's opinion. It's understandable. After all, it's their neck that is on the line. But what has worked before isn't the same as what's *possible*. What worked before has no guarantee of working again, as cultural and consumer context changes constantly, and life moves on. So, why test and make the same ad over and over again?

What's *possible* is daring. No guts, no glory. Yes, it's a risk, but the reward could be so much greater.

Research to Invigorate

Another reason why bold creative is important today is the significance and value of earned media. Media basically falls into three groups: paid, owned, and earned. Paid is exactly as it sounds: you pay for the space. Owned are channels that don't cost you anything because you already own the assets, such as in-store signage, your website, storefronts, and the like. But the most successful campaigns excel in "earned" media, a consequence of share-worthy content—basically, free attention. Consumers will only share content that is exceptional, because that is what will get them lots of likes. The shareable, likeable content out there is mold-breaking, irreverent, and/or brave. Again, this proves that great work works. And great work comes from seeking out what is possible—not what has been done multiple times before.

To get to groundbreaking ideas, a smart, brave agency and client team need to understand how to disrupt a category with fresh work. The best way to find the insights necessary to do this is to gather exploratory research early on. This isn't about testing concepts; it's about learning as much as possible about the beliefs and behaviors of the target audience prior to writing any kind of strategy direction. A creative brief based on thorough research will be much stronger and will lead to more engaging, more relevant, more motivating work that is significantly more likely to succeed in market. The insights at the core of the work will resonate with consumers, even if the work that surrounds those insights scares them slightly.

While my department's strategic planners and I are likely to commission quantitative research (meaning online surveys, which are faster, more accurate, more robust, and cheaper) to generate new information, nothing beats talking with consumers in person. Qualitative research, in this early stage, is one of the best ways to dig deep and find hidden consumer insight.

There is a lot of confusion in our industry about the word "insight." An "insight" is not the same as a fact. For example, the (admittedly generalized) idea that "women tend to care more about car colors than men do" is simply a fact, based on statistics. I have seen it proven time and time again, in dozens of car focus groups (over the years I have worked with Audi, Mercedes-Benz, and Toyota) and in many national quantitative surveys. If this is an example of a fact based on data, what is an "insight"? According to dictionary.com:

insight • /ˈɪnˌsaɪt/
noun
1. an instance of apprehending the true nature of a thing, especially through intuitive understanding.
2. penetrating mental vision or discernment; faculty of seeing into inner character or underlying truth.
3. *Psychology.* **a.** an understanding of relationships that sheds light on or helps solve a problem. **b.** (in psychotherapy) the recognition of sources of emotional difficulty. **c.** an understanding of the motivational forces behind one's actions, thoughts, or behavior; self-knowledge.

Analyzing data can reveal a ton of useful information, but will not often lead you to insights. Data can tell you *what* people think or feel, or *how* they behave, but it cannot tell you *why* the consumer feels a certain way. Only qualitative research can bring you that degree of insight.

If we use the same car example as before, an example of a true insight would be: "women inherently understand that their car is a 'second skin' whose color is a public representation of their status or personality."

I have heard versions of these words in many interviews with 30- to 50-something female luxury car drivers. In interviews, red was synonymous with passion and freedom, and was most commonly chosen after a divorce or a significant life change. Blue represented stability and was chosen as a calming influence by those with hectic lifestyles. While somewhat stereotypical, white was considered womanly (many female real estate agents drive white cars). This tells us that while color may seem like a trite reason for choosing a car, *psychologically*, color is very significant and relevant to a woman's status, state of mind, and how she wants to be seen in the world.

For this kind of research, focus groups are still valuable, whether online or in person, but there are other useful qualitative approaches:

- 1:1 interviews, or triads (mini-focus groups of three people)

- stakeholder interviews: interviewing key clients from different disciplines to understand more about the company, its brands, and its customers (this is essential)

- shop-alongs: asking consumers to think aloud, while a moderator or the account planner accompanies them on a shopping trip, taking notes

- open-ended questions: inviting the consumer to write responses during a survey

- social listening: observing publicly available trending search questions and social posts and engagement

Social listening is the one type of research on this list that is a hybrid of qualitative and quantitative, because it provides a certain degree of national or global insight at scale. We use social listening all the time, and while it is valuable for tracking consumer sentiment and understanding what is on their minds, there are some challenges. People tend to post either very positive or very negative sentiments— rarely anything in between that might be a closer representation of their mood or attitudes. Plus, those who are the most active in social media have the loudest voices (the squeakiest wheels) and, therefore, are not necessarily representative of the audience in question, as a diverse whole.

When we conduct qualitative research, we do it across multiple states to ensure that we take regional differences into consideration. We also ensure that our recruitment is diverse, so it is more representative of the U.S. population. On any typical project covering four regions, we might conduct two focus groups per region, for example, one older and one younger, or one male and one female. Or for ethnographic interviews, at least six interviews per region. Individual focus groups last 90 minutes to 2 hours. And 1:1 ethnographies are generally less, at 1 hour per interview.

Two of my favorite qualitative research methods are worth going into in more detail: brand deprivation and ethnographies.

BRAND DEPRIVATION

Hill Holliday was an early adopter of this type of research in the mid-2000s, when the agency was working with one of our most famous clients, Dunkin' Donuts. At that time, Dunkin' (which is 100 percent franchisee-owned) was mostly known as a Massachusetts-based brand for mostly blue-collar workers, with no time to linger. The brand's biggest nemesis was Starbucks—the challenger and newer kid on the block whose national footprint was increasing daily and which was considered a superior brand experience, even if Dunkin' coffee enthusiasts believed that Dunkin' coffee tasted better.

At the time, Dunkin' was best known for the old ads featuring "Fred the Baker" uttering that oft-repeated phrase, "Time to make the donuts." Since Dunkin's focus was, and still is, primarily coffee-based beverages—not to mention the fact Fred had died—the Dunkin' marketing team wanted to reposition the brand. It was time for a new campaign direction.

Rather than conducting the usual focus groups, the team decided to conduct a deprivation exercise to understand the differences between these two highly competitive brands. A group of Dunkin' regulars were asked to forgo their daily visits for 2 weeks and, instead, go to Starbucks. A group of Starbucks aficionados were asked to do the reverse. The agency then conducted focus groups with each cohort, to discuss their experience of the long, hard 2 weeks of cheating on their beloved coffee brand. This whole exercise was repeated more recently, with very similar results.

The Starbucks enthusiasts were appalled by Dunkin'. While some admitted that the coffee was good, they hated the way they were hurriedly shuffled in and out, and missed lingering in the comfortable Starbucks easy chairs, laptops on their knees, long after the last dregs of their coffee had been drunk. They felt out of place in the stark stores, which were furnished with basic tables and chairs, and painted builders' white, with splashes of orange and pink (Dunkin' did not want people to linger). They also felt the Dunkin' clientele was a bit rough around the edges for their tastes.

The Dunkin' enthusiasts fared no better. They were traumatized by the experience. Some had not made it to the end of the 2 weeks; those who did couldn't get back to Dunkin' fast enough. They felt Starbucks was a pretentious brand for pretentious people who didn't seem to work too hard, because they seemed to have hours of free time to slowly sip on their expensive, bitter coffee, while surfing the Web and resisting actually talking to anyone else in the store. The lines were long, but no one seemed to mind waiting for their order, which was baffling to the Dunkin' group. They felt self-conscious and awkward standing around waiting for a cup of coffee.

The research was invaluable. It was clear Dunkin' and Starbucks were two distinct teams. They could peacefully coexist, but Dunkin' team members would never switch their loyalty to Starbucks and vice versa. The most valuable insight was around the Dunkin' team. The perception of Dunkin' as a blue-collar northeastern brand (although the Dunkin' footprint had expanded nationally) was not the typical profile of a challenger brand and user, but the agency saw a great opportunity. Instead of trying to appeal to a broader or more upscale audience—the mistake that brands often make and in the process, turning their backs on their identity and current audience—Dunkin' decided to lean in.

The resulting campaign positioned Dunkin' as a brand for the hardworking people who keep America running every day. People who want to get in, get out, and get on with their day. Those with blue-collar, steel-toed values, even if they wore dress shirts and wingtips. From this insight and this profile, the brand positioning, and now-famous tagline, were born: "America runs on Dunkin'." It became much more than just a tagline, however. It became and still is the North Star of the brand—influencing not only Dunkin's advertising campaigns, but also the store design, the food (everything must be handheld), the drive-through—in short, the entire brand experience. And it all started with a simple deprivation exercise, yet again proving that great research yields great insight, yields great creative briefs, resulting in great work.

This positioning and tagline speaks to Dunkin' Donuts' hardworking, die-hard users. Courtesy of Dunkin' Donuts.

We have conducted other deprivation exercises over the years, including for Verizon Wireless, where we tried to deprive teenagers of their smartphones for a week. That didn't go so well. No one made it past day 1, which, in itself, was valuable insight.

ETHNOGRAPHIES

Several years ago, while working at Merkley Newman Harty in New York City, I conducted 1:1 ethnographic interviews with luxury car drivers in four states. Ethnography respondents are recruited just as focus group respondents are—typically, through a third-party recruitment firm, with access to databases of people who have signed up to do consumer research. The agency (or client) pays a recruitment fee, as well as an incentive fee for each respondent who participates.

I was in New Jersey on a drizzly winter evening, in the home of a 40-something male Mercedes-Benz E-Class owner's home. The only other person in the room was the cameraperson. All of our research was recorded, and so the conversation went like this:

Me: This is a beautiful home.

Respondent: Thank you. We like it.

Me: Why is luxury so important to you?

Respondent (while standing next to a huge, high-end, flat-screen TV): Umm... it's not, not really... I like to be comfortable, but, er... it's not about luxury. That's not what's important to me.

Me: What's most important?

Respondent: Family is the most important thing to me (points to framed photograph of family members and talks about his wife and children).

(As it is getting dark outside, respondent stands up and makes a point of flipping on outside pool lights.)

Me: So, tell me, why did you choose the Mercedes-Benz E-Class if it's not about luxury?

Respondent: Because it's the safest car on the road, for my family.

Me: Is safety the only reason?

Respondent: It's not the only reason but it's the main reason.

(Respondent slightly loosens his tie, which he has been wearing, with a pricey suit, for the duration of the interview.)

Me: Would you consider Volvos to be safe cars?

Respondent: Well, yes, they are very safe cars. I owned a Volvo a few years ago.

Me: Why didn't you choose a Volvo this time? Why Mercedes-Benz?

Respondent: Ah, well, you have me there (laughs). Well... I did like the look of the Mercedes-Benz. It's a beautiful car.

Me: How does driving the Mercedes-Benz make you feel?

Respondent: It makes me feel good.

Me: What do you think it makes others feel or think about you, compared to what they might think about you driving the Volvo?

Respondent: Um... well... (laughs). I guess it makes them think I am quite successful.

Me: And how does that, in turn, feel to you?

Respondent: I suppose I have to admit it feels good... because I started out in life poor... and with a single mom looking after us... who really struggled... so, yes, it makes me feel proud to be successful... um... because, I guess, I wasn't supposed to be.

Me: So, in that regard, what role does Mercedes-Benz play in your life, beyond safety?

Respondent: I suppose it makes me feel successful. And if I'm honest, it makes me feel the same as the people in my neighborhood. Socially, that is.

(Respondent looks out of the window, at his Mercedes-Benz E-Class, which has been very recently washed and polished, sitting in the driveway, close to the road, not parked in his nearby garage. Respondent pushes up his tie knot.)

A lot was revealed in this one interview that wouldn't have come to the surface in quantitative research. Not just from what he said, but also from how he said it. I was able to observe his home environment, with its elements of luxury, such as the pool that he (and, presumably, his spouse) had chosen, and I was able to read his body language. These are the important nuances that you only get from qualitative research, in particular, from ethnographic research in people's homes. And those nuances lead to insight instead of mere information.

I learned an awful lot about this person and his relationship with his car. Over the course of 60 minutes, I learned that:

· even though he said that luxury wasn't important, the things around him, including the TV and the pool, confirmed that it most certainly is

· family and safety are most important to him. That was his rationale for buying an expensive luxury car. However, emotionally, he bought a Mercedes-Benz because it makes him look successful to the people around him. He parks the car close to the street, not in the garage, so it is in full view—for himself and others to observe.

· Mercedes-Benz makes him feel successful, after having grown up poor

· the Mercedes-Benz car is a self-reward for climbing up the social ladder; it says, "I made it"

· the wearing of the suit, shirt, and tie, instead of changing into casual wear in his own home, at 8 PM was, in all probability, a display of power dressing. Feeling powerful and secure as an adult are extremely desirable if you felt powerless and insecure as a child.

Each subsequent interview validated these insights and built on them. This is how it works: you use one interview to influence what you ask in the next, as you look for patterns of thought and behavior. Security was a recurring theme and, ultimately, the word "secure" became an important (single word) brief for this campaign assignment.

WHATEVER FORM OF qualitative research you conduct, the quality of the insights and the honesty of the respondents depend on the quality of the questions you ask. Ask authentic questions.

Don't waste too much time on pleasantries up front, such as, "How many cats do you have?" (For some reason, many moderators have an unnatural fixation on household pets.) The intent is to relax the respondent, but it sets up a superficial dynamic that is hard to shake off.

Don't use old-fashioned research techniques such as, "Hey, let's imagine a brand party" or asking people to "Draw what happiness looks like to you." (Incidentally, if you are interested, they will almost all draw a beach or field, with blue skies and sea, and a bright yellow sun. If you can't resist, try it and you will see this play out for yourself.)

Instead, launch into a frank discussion by asking a hard question almost immediately. They will be so taken aback, and their conscious mind will have so little time to process the question, that it will pro-voke a much more candid response and more useful discussion. This approach suggests to the respondent that "I want us to be straight with each other" and sets up an environment of honest exchange.

I know an anthropologist who sometimes moderates focus groups and does so in a unique style. A few years ago, my agency commis-sioned him to moderate focus group discussions for a blood pressure drug. The first question he asked the group, just a beat after they sat down was, "Why is life so hard these days?" He didn't ask them *if* life was hard. Because we already know that life *is* hard. Instead, he engaged them in an instantly powerful and honest conversation about the struggles they had in life and with their medical conditions. This approach yields wonderful, useable insights.

On this occasion we learned that people—men, in particular—frequently refuse to take blood pressure medication not because they are forgetful or stubborn (a superficial fact), but because it is often the first firm evidence of aging that they experience; admitting to yourself that most of your life is behind you instead of ahead of you is difficult, as is losing control over your body and health. To cope with the harshness of that fact and return agency to themselves, many respondents chose to interpret their condition as a sign they must have abused their bodies in the past, reframing high blood pressure as the consequence they deserved. But this meant that taking the drug was essentially an admission of failure and burdened them with guilt. That's a true insight.

This insight helped us reposition the drug as a treatment for something that is beyond human control. High blood pressure is typically hereditary and affects younger as well as older people. It is not something you *"do"* to yourself. We had to convince people that taking the drug was not just about health, but also about life extension—and that this was within their control. Regaining control over something that wasn't their fault in the first place was an important insight that was discovered by digging in—and not settling for superficial responses.

As this next story also illustrates, the deeper you dig with qualitative research, the better the insight, which leads to strong brand positionings and, eventually, powerful creative ideas.

A Wealth of Insight

Some years ago, I worked with a well-known investment firm with ultra-high-net-worth clients. Their primary target audience is those with more than $10 million of investable assets. The secondary targets are influencers and opinion formers. The brand had recently been acquired by a bank, and the client wanted us to create a campaign to announce this fact.

We felt that a simple announcement would be a waste of good media space. This was a chance for us to redefine the positioning of the brand, which our own consumer research told us had low awareness and familiarity among consumers. This was a big issue, because it meant no trust had been built between brand and prospective clients—and ultra-high-net-worth clients would only ever put their hard-earned fortunes in the hands of a wealth management company that had been proven as trustworthy.

The marketing team agreed to tell the story of the acquisition within the framework of a campaign that targeted a new generation of middle-aged wealthy prospects who we were calling the "working wealthy." We knew a younger version of this target from working with Smith Barney (a brand that no longer exists) in our New York office a few years previously.

The qualitative research we had done for Smith Barney told us their target was between 40 and 60 years of age, with a high net worth (between around $1 million and $10 million in investable assets), but was nowhere near retirement. In fact, this cohort told us in focus groups that they loved working so much, they had no intention of ever retiring. Work was a way for them to improve not only their net worth, but also, as they told us, their feelings of self-worth. They had typically earned their money through starting businesses from scratch. They had grown up middle class or in households where parents lived paycheck to paycheck. Now they were wealthy, but didn't see themselves as such (though, they knew they were very comfortable). They didn't understand what it meant to be affluent, what the rules of play were. This was something they had had to learn.

They were concerned about two key things. First, that their children grow up with more than they had, but not at the expense of building solid character and a strong work ethic. Second, they wanted to leave money to their children, but had no idea how much to leave without spoiling them. They wanted their kids to be comfortable, but they didn't want them to just put up their feet after the reading of the will.

In stakeholder interviews with Smith Barney financial advisors, we learned that before they asked clients about investment or retirement, or offered any kind of guidance, they conducted a rigorous process of "discovery" involving many questions about the client's employment, history, knowledge, dreams, ambitions, fears, and concerns—questions about their lives, not just their money. This was very unusual at the time.

Smith Barney had developed a genuine "culture of questions." Respondents in our qualitative research were attracted to this idea. They had high awareness of the brand but hadn't known anything about how the advisors worked differently. We realized the role of Smith Barney was not just to invest, but also to get to know clients, so they could offer them advice and guidance, to help them make the right decisions with a clear conscience.

We created an outdoor and print campaign that asked a series of provocative questions. These were the difficult kinds of questions that the working wealthy lost sleep over, and that Smith Barney had the expertise to help answer. To illustrate, one ad featuring a young teenager had this headline: "Will my child inherit the work ethic or the wealth ethic?" High-net-worth consumers recognized these questions and, as a result, felt that Smith Barney was a brand that understood modern wealth and the tension it created for newly wealthy people, like them. The campaign showed deep empathy and that, in turn, built trust and consideration.

Now, back to that investment brand for the ultra-high-net-worth group.

This legacy brand's audience was that same "working wealthy" group, but a decade or so down the line. At their current life stage (typically, late 50s through 70s), relationships and trust have been built up over a long time, making it difficult to convince someone to switch investment companies and advisors. But some do indeed switch. For example, if circumstances dramatically change (moving countries or inheriting, acquiring, or selling a company), and their current advisor is not equipped to deal with these changes, or if they sense that their money is not being handled properly, or simply because they believe that their advisor is not acting in their best interest.

For these rare switchers, recommendation and reputation are key factors that affect their choice of a new institution. Awareness and familiarity of this particular brand were low, so it was important to first demonstrate empathy with the prospective audience. We needed to reposition the brand as a wealth management company that deeply understood the audience, their personal values, and what money meant to them in the past as well as today.

To do that, we needed to rise above the generic advertising that dominates the wealth management category: older couples holding hands, walking along a beach, or scooting past on their expensive boats, hair blowing in the wind. Smiling grandchildren and the ubiquitous golden lab retriever. These ads are generic, because they are written by significantly poorer and much younger creatives who have no idea what it feels like to be extremely wealthy. And their equally young and poor account planners haven't provided them with any useful or inspiring insight, because ultra-high-net-worth people are notoriously difficult to recruit for any kind of consumer research: they do not need the one-hundred-dollar incentive, and they do not have the time or motivation to attend a focus group or ethnographic interview. Because of this, planners tend to rely on secondary research; the personal experiences of older, affluent friends or relatives; or plain assumption and unvalidated hypotheses. All far, far from ideal, as you can tell by the generic results.

Generic work advertises the category, not the brand. You can likely guess which category this image represents. dmbaker/Depositphotos.

There is a saying that account planners have used for decades: "You don't have to be the audience to understand the audience." But you can only understand the audience if you can talk to enough of them. We needed to engage the audience in qualitative research, so we could find an insight to drive better work. This is where having Karen Kaplan (who is now Hill Holliday's chairman and CEO) as your boss comes in very handy.

Karen has a contact list the length of the Charles River. She made some personal calls to some influential, wealthy people, and we were able to set up about two dozen interviews with ultra-high-net-worth individuals in the northeast (NE), the west, and the south. We were against the clock, as the media had already been bought (yes, that happens all the time), so we conducted the interviews in the NE in person and the others by phone. I conducted these interviews myself, along with one of my most senior strategic planners, and was insistent on doing in-home interviews for all the reasons I outlined in my Mercedes-Benz example from before. Context is everything. Nuances, body language, and subtleties are all incredibly important, and this is often where the magic lies.

Doing in-home interviews with wealthy people is fascinating. You are met at the door by a member of "staff" (in one case, what I assumed was a butler, and in many of the others, a housekeeper), their homes are incredible, and you are offered high-end snacks and refreshments that looked like petits fours—a far cry from the peanuts and M&M's one is offered at many focus group facilities. Unlike regular homes, where it's difficult to squeeze in the cameraperson as well as yourself, in wealthy people's homes, the challenge is finding an intimate corner in the vast rooms where a megaphone isn't needed to have a chat. We did our best, settled in for the interviews, and gained insights that were absolutely fascinating.

These folks told us that aside from winning the lottery, playing the markets, or becoming a celebrity, there are three principal ways of becoming extremely wealthy:

1. climb the corporate ladder to CEO, which means a big sign-on bonus, paycheck, annual bonus, lots of valuable stock, and a huge golden parachute (do that more than once and you are loaded)

2. inherit a ton of cash from your family, or marry rich (rare)

3. inherit or start a business, build it, and sell it (some had done this two or three times)

Most of them fell into bucket number 3, and their industries ranged from chemical engineering to tech companies to video empires. As the interviews continued over a 2-week period, common traits started to emerge, such as:

- Perseverance: in some instances, their businesses had failed. When asked what happened next, we were told that "you dust yourself off and start over until you succeed."

- Goal-oriented: when asked, "Why not just give up?" they said that being driven is a blessing and a curse, that they were constantly trying to achieve a goal, no matter what. Not having a goal was disconcerting to them, so when they achieved a goal they immediately set a new goal. The thrill was in the chase—not the prize.

- Achievements over possessions: the trappings of wealth were of secondary importance. Yes, a lovely home, nice cars, and a boat or two were great, but the sense of achievement that seemed to validate their sense of self-worth was more important.

- Emotional: A surprising number of tears were shed during these interviews, as they recalled, for example, the intense pressure of a failure (especially when the business had been inherited), or not being present enough for their spouse or children, or a difficult childhood, or highly influential and now deceased parents.

- Social mobility: Surprised that these driven people were not more self-confident, we probed them about their early years. Each and every one had grown up working or middle class. Most of their parents had either never had enough money or lived paycheck to paycheck. Some came from extreme poverty.

- Insecure: Most had gone to university through scholarships and had struggled with a sense of inferiority compared to classmates from wealthy families.

- Boomers: Most were in their 60s and had fully experienced the free love era of the 1970s.

- Isolation: Most felt they didn't belong anywhere other than in their immediate families. Their old friends and extended families had not achieved anywhere near the same level of wealth, so they had little in common with them, and many did not trust or click with their peer groups.

- Unassuming: it would be impossible to pick each from a crowd based on appearances; they dressed well, but casually. They looked like everyone else—wealth doesn't look the way you expect it to.

Most important to us, each displayed an emblem or other reminder of their humble beginnings, whether it was on their desk, wall, or credenza. For one person, it was a picture of his immigrant mother. For another, it was a pebble from the beach near their childhood home. We saw a photograph of a man's first apartment, and a framed copy of a woman's first paycheck. When asked about these mementos, they replied that no matter how well they did in life, they never wanted to forget where they had come from—even if their start in life was difficult or painful.

When we returned to the office, I asked my team to research what percentage of wealth in the USA was self-made. It seemed unusual that all of these wealthy interviewees came from humble beginnings. Coming from the more rigid class system in the UK, I felt that this must have been a coincidence. My team came back with robust numbers: between 80 and 90 percent of wealthy people in the U.S. described their wealth as self-made. I made them recheck this, and, sure enough, the statistics were correct. This was mind-blowing to me—I couldn't believe that no competitive brand out there was talking about this in any of their advertising. But, then again, as I mentioned before, few had been able to get personal audiences with these ultra-wealthy individuals.

All of this convinced us that this investment firm had a great and unique opportunity. Most of the ultra-high-net-worth folks we spoke to were extremely intimidated by and suspicious of traditional financial services companies, which illustrate "old money" and a dusty approach to wealth management. These companies and their advertising—which showed the traditional trappings of wealth and retirement, the wood-paneled walls and the luxury cars—did not speak to our audience, or their personal values, at all.

Our audience was still active in their businesses and were more motivated by their journey and their goals. They never wanted to lose touch with who they were. They really were different. And so was the brand. It worked with those more traditional consumers, but stakeholder interviews showed that it also employed many advisors with a contemporary outlook and approach who were experts in helping those with sudden or newer wealth. These advisors understood that just because someone is wealthy, doesn't mean they are self-directed when it comes to investing. Whether their brains weren't wired to understand how to invest or they were too busy doing what they do well—or both—they needed help.

The brand positioning we created was simple:

A different kind of investment company
for a different kind of investor.

The campaign that sprung from this proposition and creative brief pushed against the category conventions. Rather than showing old wealth retiring into a sedentary lifestyle punctuated by the occasional game of golf or quick spin in the new yacht (and, of course, that walk on the beach with their loved one), our ads featured still-working ultra-high-net-worth individuals next to their prized possessions—and not one of these was the trappings of wealth. We showed the things that were important to them and that kept them grounded: the house where they were raised, their first car, the diner they loved to eat in when they were young (and still did).

The intensive qualitative research had resulted in genuine, new insights. The resulting campaign felt fresh, different, and authentic. Prospects agreed: not long after the campaign launch, lead generation increased significantly, and we received touching and appreciative letters (yes, actual letters) and e-mails from ultra-high-net-worth people who loved the campaign, because they had recognized themselves and their own stories in the ads. When very wealthy and busy people lift a pen to write a note about an ad, that ad must really have touched a nerve. This campaign serves as another reminder that good research generates powerful insights into the consumer mind-set, which in turn informs the creative brief. And if the work is on brief, it will typically perform well after launch.

SIX

Data and the Science of Strategic Planning

IN THE EARLY DAYS of advertising, until about a decade or so ago, the "art" of advertising was felt to be enough. An ad would win awards if it looked like a 60-second movie. That ad may have looked and felt amazing, but it didn't always move the needle, and if it did, it was often by chance. Those days are over.

The single biggest shift in the use of research in our industry over the last decade is the sheer proliferation and use of data. All clients talk about today is data: the importance of data. The need for data. Data-infused insights. Data-informed solutions. The mantra "digital or die" has become "data or die." If today's planners and agencies are not data literate, they will not survive.

All this data can be incredibly overwhelming. When abused, it can hurt. When used properly, it is a beautiful thing.

The ability to form a complete data loop is a critical part of the success of any modern agency. At my company, pulling D&A into the core agency from its origins as a media-only function has been a very,

very successful change for us. It demonstrated that the role of data extends well beyond media monitoring and optimization. Modern strategic planners, with their data analyst partners, need to help our clients understand the key role data can play in identifying business and consumer opportunities, through testing and learning and performance analytics. Planners need to navigate the whole data loop across the entire customer experience, *without* killing great ideas.

Why is this so important? Clients do not pay agencies a huge amount of money to think and approach problems in the same way that they do. They pay us to challenge them and think differently. They pay us for creative excellence. They want us to suggest new ideas and solutions by using the less analytical right side of our brains. But the stakes have never been higher (think of the average tenure of a CMO or CEO), and the tolerance for trial and error shrinks every quarter. The role of agencies today, and particularly strategic planners, is to strike the right balance of inspiring creative and reassuring data. Data is critical to support creative, but we can't overcorrect and stifle new ideas. Data must provide insight and evidence that helps new ideas survive and thrive, so that the art and science of our craft are both represented throughout the process of creating advertising.

Creative is still king. And ad agencies still attract the best creative talent, despite the competition from in-house agencies; or consulting firms like Accenture, which provide rigor (and that have even gobbled up ad agencies); or big tech Alpha brands like Google, Apple, and Facebook. Why? Creative people want to work in a creative environment, with people who share a purpose, passion, and vision, which is to make amazing, effective work that they can be proud of. Also, brilliant creative people, who generally have short attention spans, do not want to spend all of their time working on one brand. And once they jump to the client or in-house or consultancy side, their portfolios will lack variety, so the longer their tenure, the harder it is to get back to the agency world. (Yes, consulting firms do work on multiple brands, but advertising is not their core expertise, so the culture of the company may be less desirable.) Most great creatives want to work at great agencies to keep themselves interested and engaged, and to keep their portfolios fresh.

Will that change in future? In all probability, it may, especially as marketing budgets continue to get squeezed, and the competition offers more attractive packages. But for the foreseeable future, I believe that ad agencies will continue to attract the best talent. However, no matter how great the talent and how great the creative, it will never be enough for today's clients.

The work simply has to work.

If the work dazzles audiences, but doesn't lead to measurable business results, CMOs will take the client's business elsewhere (assuming they keep their job). Long gone are the legacy client agency relationships of 10 or 20 years or more. Clients today are nervous, and that makes them fickle, so agencies need to stay disciplined and ahead of the curve, looking out for every potential obstacle and opportunity.

When used well and selectively, data gives us a significantly greater chance of helping the work to work. It helps us understand our consumers better. It helps us determine what drives their emotions, behaviors, and decisions as they move through the path to purchase. It helps us to optimize positionings, ideas, and media channels and track the effectiveness of not only media choices, but also brand and business metrics. Data also gives us the ability to launch great, mold-breaking ideas, knowing that we have done everything in our power to help them, and our clients, be successful.

The Data Loop

When any agency is pitching for a piece of new business or planning a new or evolved strategic and creative direction for an existing brand, the strategic planner is at the center of the process, using research and data to inform and inspire themselves and others on the team. There are many stages, all relying on research and data: analyzing business data to help define what success looks like; finding consumer insight; testing positioning territories; pretesting creative concepts; doing in-market testing, such as AB testing; tracking brand and creative success; analyzing media effectiveness; and, ultimately, establishing if the team has met the KPIs of success.

It's a cyclical process that is informed by a data loop, which, sadly, is not approached with this degree of rigor nearly enough, partially because not all agencies have the ideal conditions. To complete a data loop, it is best if:

- your agency has an in-house media team to plan and buy the client's media

- your agency has an in-house decision science (D&A/research) team to help you plan and analyze the use of data

- your agency is owned by a holding company and has access to their data and tech capabilities, such as IPG's Acxiom and Kinesso (although, typically, access isn't free—you have to pay to play, in one way or another)

- you have media autonomy; that is, there is no pressure to partner with your client's media team. If that's the case, they will have a vested interest in keeping the data from you. After all, data is power. Agencies do not like exposing one another to their proprietary tools, processes, and approaches, lest they be stolen (and, of course, they will be).

- your client has integrated brand, digital, and/or social capabilities. Why any smaller or mid-sized brand would split these into different agencies is beyond me, as it is totally inefficient. For large clients and brands, the desire for specialization is understandable, but it's not easy to execute—the separate agencies do not really like working with one another, as hard as they might try to get along.

- your client is not in a highly regulated industry, such as banking or pharmaceuticals, where privacy is paramount and data cannot be shared

Let's assume that you do have in-house media (or an unusually fantastic relationship with your sister media agency). Where do you start, and where does data play a role?

The following approach is what I have found to be most successful when planning a brand launch or campaign. You do not need to go

The use of data and research when planning advertising

- Business analytics and market assessment; financial statement analysis and modeling in support of KPI development
- Competitive intelligence
- Key driver analysis and market sizing
- Client data analysis

- Cultural analysis
- Consumer research and journey mapping
- Perceptual mapping
- Brand family mapping
- Customer segment valuations
- Analysis of syndicated research
- Social listening
- Lifetime value (LTV), propensity, and look-alike modeling

Business & Competitive Analysis

Cultural, Consumer, & Brand Analysis

Strategy Development

Creative/Channel Execution

Performance & Improvement

- Program attribute, positioning, messaging research (conjoint, discrete choice, etc.)
- Pre-market testing
- Forecasting performance against KPIs

- Brand tracking
- Descriptive analytics and reporting, including sales tracking and visualizations
- In-market measurement and optimization against KPIs and testing (e.g., AB tests)

- Market opportunity analysis, budget allocation, and flighting simulations
- Uplift modeling/analysis
- Dashboard development
- Data creation, collection, cleaning, and reporting
- MarTech infrastructure assessment

Data and research inform the work, which leads to more research and more data, which informs the work…

through this entire process for each and every brief campaign, only for significant new brand or campaign changes that will last for several years. "America runs on Dunkin'," for example, has been the brand's tagline for over 14 years now, and I do not see it changing anytime soon—even if the context and campaigns around it evolve to remain relevant, as culture and consumer beliefs and behaviors progress over time.

If the process looks lengthy, let me reassure you, it is not, and it cannot be. Done well, with the right team, each stage happens simultaneously with teams sharing their findings almost in real time. This whole process should take at least several weeks ideally, but it can take as little as 5–10 days, including proprietary research, if expedited. Clients do not have the patience or budgets for things to drag, so the more skilled you become at this type of planning work, the faster it will move, without sacrificing quality. Your clients will be happy, and so will your creatives—they are not going to let you take half or more of a 6-week total timeline to do your strategy work, while they are left with a paltry week or so to do the actual creative work.

However, a word of caution: as tempting as it is to expedite, do not rush this *if at all possible*. A new brand house, tagline, or big brand campaign idea is a big deal. It will significantly affect the future of the brand, so unless it is an emergency, don't shortchange your clients or your team. Give this the attention it deserves, and it will yield great dividends.

The account planner needs to lead the charge and make it all happen. Throughout the process, data plays a critical role, informing, giving insight, validating hypotheses (or not), providing analytical rigor, all while ensuring that ideas remain intact or are enhanced by data.

The KPIs of Success

Advertising is not a magic bullet; one campaign rarely transforms a client's business. But a good campaign should be able to create measurable change. The first part of the process is establishing how to measure that change, and what success will look like.

Do not skip this part, no matter how tempting to you and/or your clients. I know it's exciting to get to the consumer insight work and write a juicy brief for the creatives, but if you skip this step it will be impossible to gauge your success. You will also ultimately waste time: endless hours will be spent spinning, debating strategy and creative, because you have no objectives against which to judge the work. It will come down to personal opinion. Or, should I say, opinions. Because there is never only one of them.

If the KPIs for success are not immediately available, do not give up. Even if clients are resisting because they want to get moving, you must insist on doing this work. Of course, herein lies the rub: there is a vulnerability in establishing KPIs, because they can establish failure as well as success. But isn't it better to work with the benchmark or foundation of real metrics?

Frequently, agencies are given goals that are soft brand metrics, such as increasing brand awareness or consideration. While these are important, what you need to push for are specific business goals. Are online sales declining due to cheaper competition? If off-line sales are weak in a region, how can advertising reasonably help, and what level of investment would be needed to do so? What goal can advertising credibly help achieve? What other activations are happening in that region other than advertising? Is your KPI for success stealing a percentage of the share from a competitor? If so, what percentage share seems reasonable, based on past data and media spend?

Sometimes the marketing team says they cannot find the relevant data or they do not understand their data. I guarantee there is someone within the organization who *can* find it, and who does understand it. Find that person, pull in your account leads and analytics team, and work with them (and the marketing team if they will jump in) to figure out what needs to be done and how advertising can help.

If this person does not exist (it's rare, but it happens), then ask your client if they are willing (and legally able) to share any data, so that you can crunch the numbers with the help of your decision science team. If they cannot share data, you may have to rely on what's publicly available. There is plenty of it out there, and it brings at least some rigor to the process. And if you are part of a holding company and are lucky enough to have access to its data stack, then go at it. For the purpose of illustration, I will assume that this is not the case (the reality for most small to mid-sized agencies).

If your brand is seriously outspent by the competition, then your client's expectations need to be fair. You cannot claim the number one slot if you are outspent 10:1. You will only have a rat's chance in hell of doing so *if* the product and brand are updated or transformed in preparation for relaunch, *and* you create a radical, risky campaign that is polarizing but that gets talked about. That's the adrenaline shot that can either cure you or kill you. Few clients today have the stomach for such a big risk unless the brand is a seriously Old Dog, in which case, it will probably be your last hope to avoid putting it to sleep for good.

One great KPI that proves effectiveness robustly and quickly is a media test. In-market tests, such as those conducted by Google Ads (to optimize digital ad content), provide speedy results and are much simpler to conduct. However, for omnichannel campaigns, if all other variables are more or less equal (distribution, demographics, the level of spend on any other promotional activities), then comparing sales in a region where a campaign ran against sales in another region where the campaign did not run is the purest way to establish effectiveness (or if you are unlucky, ineffectiveness). You can also use this type of test to determine how the combination of brand and retail messages in one region compared to a similar region, with the same spend, where only retail messages ran. Trying to justify brand advertising in a tough economy is very, very hard. Soft metrics won't cut it, so, where possible, opt for a media test. Nothing motivates a CEO more than seeing the effect of advertising on actual sales.

Another reason for rigor when it comes to business metrics is that often, and especially today, advertising spend is one of the first things to be cut when a CEO is trying to reduce costs. If the CMO cannot prove the effectiveness of the advertising, they cannot fight these cuts. Establishing and reaching the KPIs for success are the only ways to protect the budget. Media tests put the client in a strong position to justify the spend, but don't wait until the budget is threatened to run the test. Be armed and ready with the data in advance. It's a subtle but important difference. When asked to justify spend, don't argue for retaining or finding more money to roll out a successfully tested campaign—instead, turn the message around and present the CEO with the numbers that represent the potential financial consequence of *not* rolling out the campaign. FOMO is often a key motivator.

Finally, and critically, in my experience, if the business goals and objectives of the campaign are generic or unclear as the campaign is being developed, no one, including the creatives, will understand what the work is supposed to be doing. Without KPIs, the client is making decisions about the work based on whether or not it appeals to them personally—and that makes no sense whatsoever. How is a client who is (typically) middle-aged and (frequently) conservative supposed to judge if a campaign for a Gen Z audience will succeed?

Asking a client to be more diligent about business metrics may be time consuming and there may be pushback, but if you do not do this, campaign after campaign will be rejected by the client based on personal judgments. Money and resources will be wasted, and it will steal weeks from the schedule.

Business Analysis

Well done—you have established what success will look like. Next, immerse yourself in the category and in your clients' business by reading reports from as many reliable and recent sources as you can find. Don't just rely on the opinion of one person who wrote one article back in 2016. Dig into as much reputable secondary research as you can, and ask your clients to provide you with any research and other information that they are willing to share.

For public companies, a lot can be learned by listening to earnings calls and reading annual reports. The questions asked on earnings calls force the brand leadership to think on their feet, and the nature of the questions typically gives you a lot of clues about the kinds of weaknesses and opportunities the company may be facing. You can also check stock fluctuations over the last 1–10 years, being sure to pay particular attention to the highest and lowest points and asking what was happening at the time of these peaks and troughs. Overall, is the company growing? Does it have positive momentum or not?

Best of all, try to interview the C-Suite and other stakeholders. Ask the marketing team for a list of people within the organization who can give you a broad but clear picture of the company and its brand(s). Call or meet with these people and ask why and when their business began, who the founders were, what gap the company or brand filled at that time, how successful the company has been over time. Has the company grown through acquisitions and mergers or has it grown organically? Mergers and acquisitions can result in a culture clash, which can create an unclear or confusing brand purpose, mission, and positioning. If that's the case, it will need to be addressed.

Find out who these stakeholders believe the competition is; this may have changed dramatically over the years. Note that the predominant competition isn't necessarily another company or brand. It can be a much stronger human force, such as inertia or lack of relevance.

Speak to external industry experts. Find them via your LinkedIn contacts or network with your team to find out who their relevant connections are. (Just be sure not to speak to any competitors still working in the industry!) There are many recently retired CEOs and C-Suite (and other) executives who will talk to you for a reasonable fee.

Cultural Analysis

Let's assume you now have solid, client-approved business and campaign goals and you've done all of the groundwork. Pin that information on the wall of your online or real-world war room, so that everyone has access to it, and turn your attention to the next phase, which is radically different: cultural analysis.

Culture plays a huge role in brand success or lack of success, though its significance is often overlooked or dismissed as a "soft" metric. When it comes to brands, relevance is everything. If a company or brand is not culturally relevant, then it is not relevant to consumers and simply cannot succeed.

Examine the key cultural shifts or trends in the world and in your country. There are many resources for cultural trend analysis, including subscriptions with companies that specifically track trend data. However, because these are typically pricey, and because things are moving so fast, it's important to track culture on a real-time basis, not quarterly. The latter is useful for big, broad, slow-moving cultural shifts that have taken over a year to develop, such as a downtrend in the housing market, but important trends can shift dramatically within a 24-hour period. Think of how the stock market reacts to the announcement of a corporate scandal or a new CEO of a public company. Or how COVID-19 changed everything, everywhere, in only a few days.

All cultural trends are connected, and the Internet has given us literally millions of data sources for trend analysis. Look at readily available economic data, stock market data, the housing market, customer sentiment reports, Google search trend data, fashion trends, the most popular movies and TV shows, the global news, the biggest trends in music and hobbies. Again, it is key to ensure that your sources are reliable. But the real skill is in finding the links between trends—they are always connected—and identifying in their earliest stages the trends that will endure.

These incipient trends are often the result of what is called a "cultural collision." For example, I believe that the recent surge in popularity of historical dramas—see the massive popularity of shows like *Downton Abbey*, *Outlander*, *The Last Kingdom*, and *Vikings*—may be a reaction to a significant cultural collision. Stress is always present in our culture, but over the last decade it has been compounded due to economic instability, job insecurity and overwork, overexposure to excessive information, the obsession with social media, and the pressure to be perfect. As an antidote to this stress, what could be a better than the short-term escape of binging on a good English Edwardian romp or a heroic Scottish or Viking drama—all set in a time without Internet or cell phones or social media? These trends then cause cultural shifts. The adoption of the Viking trend, for example, leads to the uptick in tribal tattoos, partially shaved heads, or funky facial hair. And this trend, in turn, conveniently responds to the fear of homogenization experienced by second-wave Millennials (the younger end of the generation) and Gen Zers. When everyone has access to the same social platforms, fashion websites, and celebrities, younger people who hate the idea of looking like everyone else will pounce on a chance to be more individual.

Any brand that anticipated this collision by carefully watching cultural trends could prepare for the associated threats or opportunities well in advance of an upturn or downturn in sales. The fashion for shaved heads and facial hair, for example, could mean a reduction in the demand for standard razors, but an increase in the demand for clippers and beard-grooming products. This illustrates that cultural trends are not "soft" metrics at all. Anticipating them and responding to them early can make sound business sense.

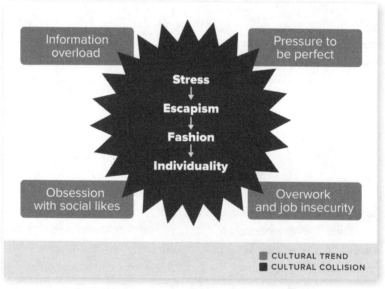

To be relevant, brands need to sense and respond to cultural collisions.

As previously mentioned, all cultural trends are connected, and there are many more I could cite that could be added to the diagram on page 100, but this illustrates my point. Four shifts contribute to one collision, and a subsequent ripple effect of needs and solutions.

So, back to brands. If your brand can respond to an early collision or trend, it will forever be connected to that trend. This will position it as a progressive and relevant brand, and, with luck, will force other brands to recalibrate to its dominance. This kind of forward momentum is a key indicator of brand energy and, therefore, success, so it is not to be underestimated.

Look how quickly Airbnb changed the world of travel accommodation. It was founded in 2008 and within a decade surpassed Hilton in U.S. sales. How did this happen? There's little doubt that Airbnb latched on to some significant early cultural shifts and trends that were emerging and that are still happening today:

- the breakdown of community in our culture is creating a sense of loss and disconnection, and a need for a sense of belonging

- hotels around the world are increasingly generic. Intrepid, cultured travelers want the unique, immersive experience offered by a real local resident's actual home.

- for these discerning travelers it is important to feel, even if for just a short time, a sense of place, rather than feeling like a tourist

- as people travel more for work and leisure, millions of rooms and homes across the globe are empty at any given time

These types of trends can be discovered or substantiated by secondary category data that is freely available. Travel and category sales data are available from sources such as statista.com or travel.trade.gov, and reliable psychology data can be found at psychologytoday.com. Resources are endless, so dig in. If you have a hunch about a trend, don't act on it until you find data to substantiate it. If the data suggests that your hunch is a growing trend—even if it is in its infancy—use it and find other trends that may be connected to it.

Remember: there are always connections! For example, a recession affects the housing market, which affects consumer security, which provokes consumer anxiety, which affects their spending. You get the gist.

It is important to act quickly. Don't dawdle and wait until the trend is mainstream—by then it will be a category convention, useless to any brand looking to challenge the status quo. If this happens, start the process over again, and next time, act sooner.

Having identified all of these trends, Airbnb positioned itself right in the center of their collision point. It created a community where each member—renter or owner—feels a sense of place and belonging. From this, they created their (abbreviated) brand purpose and tagline, "Belong anywhere." (This was inspired by Douglas Atkin, the ultimate OG planner, who was their global head of community at the time—and, more recently, the author of the Foreword to this book.)

When Airbnb claimed this cultural space, competitors such as vrbo.com, which had been around for decades already, reacted by changing their visual identity, positioning, and advertising in order to compete. But they were too slow. Airbnb recognized these significant and relevant trends early, acted on them, and owned them. Airbnb is now the world's largest online marketplace for lodgings, with listings growing more than 100 percent each year (prepandemic). Again, these are not soft metrics. That's the power of purpose and cultural relevance.

Once cultural shifts have been analyzed to give you a strong sense of the cultural territory your brand may occupy and own, the rest is fairly straightforward. The cultural context becomes the foundation of the brand campaign for everything that follows.

Competitive Analysis

Healthy Alpha brands, Youth brands, and even Newborn brands *cannot* succeed if they rely on looking for good old-fashioned "white space." Instead, it's important for these brands to lead by rising up and out of the category and look for a higher order purpose and positioning, which can only be done if they attach themselves to relevant cultural shifts or collisions.

Understanding a brand's place in the world also helps avoid stepping into another brand's territory. When that happens, differentiation is impossible, and misattribution of advertising impact to the category leader is probable.

However, analysis of the competition is necessary to understand category dynamics, including strengths, weaknesses, opportunities, and threats; the leaders, challengers, followers, and losers; as well as the strategic and creative areas to avoid—the spaces that have already been filled. The strategic planner will work with their team to immerse themselves in the category in order to:

- study how the category is broken down in terms of share—where do the brands fall in the pecking order? Is there a clear Alpha? Has leadership switched over the years? Who are the challengers, and what is their rate of growth?

- establish how each brand falls into the brand family outlined earlier

- look for any known brand assets, such as brand purpose and positioning

- review all recent advertising campaigns across all channels, over the last 5 years

- analyze category media spends, over the last 5 years, including how it is broken down by channel into TV, digital, paid social, direct response television (DRTV), out-of-home (OOH), etc.

- search for patterns; for example, in the insurance category, a handful of clear leaders spends in excess of $100 million per year, followed by a huge gap, then a tight cluster of small competitors who are fighting for scraps, with national spends of $5 million or less

This type of competitive breakdown will also help you understand the conventions within a category, an unfortunate fact of modern advertising. The skittish client and agency will try to follow convention in order to avoid making ripples—positive or negative ones. Better to keep your head below the water and allow others to take risks, according to this "do no harm" mentality—which, ironically, is a sure-fire path to mediocrity. I'll avoid the usual clichés of "sea of sameness" or "zig when others zag" (well, it seems I didn't avoid them after all), but the point I am making is that you need to fight to elevate your client above the aforementioned mediocrity. If the planner puts rigor behind the process and uses data throughout, to help protect and evolve great ideas, the work has an excellent chance of succeeding and achieving its goals after launch.

An important tool that I use for both competitive and brand analysis (later in this chapter) is perception mapping. These are not brand maps, where the axis and position of brands are based on subjective opinions, which results in team arguments about where exactly brands should be placed. These are data-informed maps, developed through quantitative research: consumers are offered a list of brands and a list of attributes and asked to pair them. The lists can include just about anything, including car brands, hotel brands, beer brands, animals, and even types of relationships.

As an example, the perception map on page 105 pairs technology brands with adjectives. It shows that Xerox is not associated with any specific attribute today, other than a distant connection to "powerful," which is probably a residual from the past. On the other hand, Hewlett Packard (HP) is considered "visionary," and Canon, "straightforward," which all make sense. The map also highlights the neutrality of the Canon brand (not a terrible thing), highlighting the need to link it to a positive attribute, which will help it stay competitive.

This may sound like an eccentric technique, but I have used these survey-based maps for many years, and similar patterns always emerge, which is reassuring. This isn't pure science, but it is a useful way to prompt consumers, in a method akin to free association, to react without thinking, which reveals brand associations, honestly.

These maps can include multibrand clusters from a variety of categories, to see how they fare alongside your brand. For example,

Perception Map

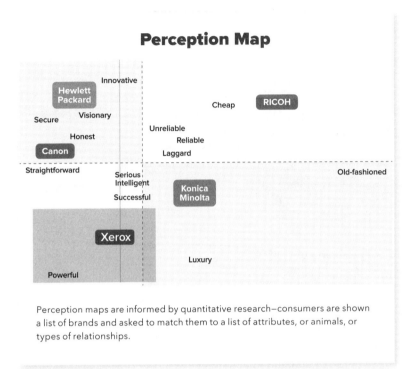

Perception maps are informed by quantitative research—consumers are shown a list of brands and asked to match them to a list of attributes, or animals, or types of relationships.

in many perception maps, I have seen Walmart be linked to Ford, Courtyard by Marriott, and Budweiser. For perception maps about relationships, I have seen it fall under "marriage of convenience" on many occasions—when the most desirable relationship status for most brands would be either "married for life" or "forbidden affair."

Let's be honest: another huge benefit of perception maps is that they are fun to present and discuss, making them good pitch or meeting theater. I once presented a famous luxury-car brand team with an animal perception map, where Chevrolet was represented by an eagle, and Mini, the upstart challenger, was represented by a rabbit (this happens a lot with small challengers). The team was horrified to see their aggressive brand represented by a shark.

To me, the shark space is the most fascinating of all, particularly for a car brand: while it is aggressive and terrifying, it is also powerful, sleek, the most perfectly evolved animal in the ocean—and, most importantly, it cannot swim backwards. Now, does the consumer pick the shark because they are aware of its associations with powerful, forward momentum? Of course not. But the subconscious is a very interesting thing—it can immediately access all the knowledge and associations we have stored since birth and it is incapable of rational thought—so, who are we to judge it?

Much like the brand family maps, perception mapping can give you not only a sense of the space the brand occupies on the consumer's mind today, but also where they need to move to, to stand up and stand out.

Consumer Analysis

Okay, so we understand the KPIs of success, we know our business challenges and goals, and we have a good sense of the general area that we want to inhabit in the culture, and the brand associations that we already own and need to own. We know a lot at this point, but we need to learn more. We need to know as much as we can about the most important part of the whole equation—the consumer.

Again—the most significant role any strategic planner plays is to represent the consumer (or customer, if you are working with B2B audiences) in the brand development or communications campaign.

Why does the consumer need to be represented in the first place? Because clients and agencies are immersed in their brands and businesses, and they spend an unhealthy amount of energy and time on both. That is their job and their livelihood. But the consumer is the most important stakeholder. Is the consumer wandering around thinking about packaged cheese or insurance plans all day long? It's highly unlikely, unless they are seriously quirky, so it is our job to ensure they are present throughout the process, so that the work is relevant, meaningful, and motivating. You may not be your target's generation, gender, or ethnicity, but you can step into their shoes for a while. Learn about their lives and their worlds. Their hopes and aspirations. Their struggles and fears. Learn what drives them.

Most importantly, learn to like them. I was once told by a very famous ECD that my brief left him disliking the affluent, middle-aged male audience whom we were trying to target. This was particularly uncomfortable since he himself was an affluent, middle-aged male. He told me that he couldn't write a campaign for someone whom he disliked, so, irritated and scratching my head, I revisited the brief, wondering how my 28-year-old self could even begin to climb into the brain of someone with whom I had absolutely nothing in common.

I had to admit to myself that I had come to the original briefing ill prepared. I hadn't done my homework and I didn't really know this audience—I had just blindly accepted our client's request to target them. I realized it was time to do what I should have done in the first place: the work. I read a lot of secondary research and psychology white papers and interviewed as many men from within this demographic as I could in the time given.

Sure enough, some themes started to emerge. At the time, the UK was going through a small recession. This was quite a while ago, when we were not as enlightened as we are today, so most family structures we focused on were fairly stereotypical, with a primary male breadwinner, female secondary breadwinner, or stay-at-home mom, with 2.5 kids. I learned that this generation of white-collar boomer men had been raised by parents who had grown up during the war. Their folks had to make every penny stretch and in their frugality had "deprived" them of many of the things their children had wanted. Two decades later, their middle-aged sons, in particular, wanted to compensate their families for the "sins" of the parents, by providing them with a nice home, nice cars, a good school, and all the right clothes, gadgets, and toys. But this stuff costs a lot of money, and they had frequently overstretched themselves, living beyond their means by relying on credit cards and the hopes of a raise.

They lived with constant worry about money. I learned that many had hidden this from their partners and spouses, shouldering the burden alone. Unlike women of a similar age, these men did not talk to their friends or families about their woes. Anyway, most of their friends were, they told us, in exactly the same situation. I also had to remember that these people had been young once. In this case, during the 1970s, when the sexual revolution was in full swing. The white-collar lives of feigned privilege that they were living now, where material possessions seemed to be important, was in direct contrast to the truly meaningful lives they had once assumed and hoped they would have.

While I had little sympathy for them regarding their financial irresponsibility, there was a loneliness and vulnerability about them that I found sad but endearing. There was also something kind of cool about them and their hippie youths that I hadn't noticed before. I learned that I actually did like them—and was then able to empathize enough to write a much better, more inspiring brief. My ECD agreed.

If you don't know your audience, do the work. It always pays off.

When you believe that you know enough, turn your attention to your audience's relationship with the category and your brand. It isn't our job to force consumers to think about brands. It is our job to encourage them to think about our brand *first*, whenever they are making decisions in the category—even if that is a year from now. We can encourage this predisposition *only* if we are seen to align with their needs and their values. A consumer chooses Dunkin' over Starbucks because they believe they belong to one "team" more than the other. And how do they pick a team? They pick the one that they *buy into* on a deeper level, even if they think they are responding to messaging about a new flavor of fall coffee. That kind of retail messaging engages consumers in the moment, but brand messaging engages them for the long term. To attract consumers to your brand, you need both types of messaging. Or at the very least, that *phrase de jour*, "branded retail"—a hybrid of a brand-oriented campaign with a heavy retail component, such as a car video with a dealer tag at the end, including details such as price, offer, and the call to action.

How does this help account planners as we plan a brand's positioning or advertising? It reminds us that an optimal level of engagement comes from understanding our consumer as deeply as we possibly can. Not only their mindset, but also their attitudes and behaviors in life, in the category and towards your brand. The *who*, *what*, and *why*. *Who* they are, *what* they think of the category and your brand, and *why* they think this.

Let's start with the who.

FINDING EXISTING CUSTOMERS

Today's clients have limited budgets, to the extent that it is not unusual to be working with a national media and production budget of less than $5 million annually. As budgets shrink, agencies need to become smarter. Insurance companies with $200 million annual budgets can afford to target pretty much everyone who might buy insurance (so, any adult) across all 50 states. These brands can afford to take risks on highly irreverent campaigns featuring animals and cavemen, not only because they are in a very low interest category, but also because if one idea bombs, it's not the end of the world—they just pull it and redistribute the spend to the more successful ads that are in the market. And, of course, they can afford to produce several ad campaigns and indeed, they have to, because ads do ultimately wear out. After too much exposure, the consumer tires of seeing the same execution, resulting in irritation and the dreaded diminishing returns. It's best to avoid this at all costs—but it is a luxury problem most brands don't have.

Overexposure is not the issue for the majority of campaigns. Usually, we have to be extremely selective on behalf of our clients, focusing on certain regions and specific demographics. There are several means of delving into audience demographics: customer databases, syndicated research, proprietary online surveys, social media, or quantitative or qualitative research. Or work with your media partners, who can collaborate with Google and Facebook to identify your best customers. And, again, if you are lucky enough to have access to your holding company's data stack, start there.

For the average planner at the average-sized agency, it makes sense to learn about a brand's best customers first. By obtaining this demographic, psychographic, and behavioral data, you can target copycat audiences who have access to your clients' brand but who, for whatever reason, do not buy or use it. Surprisingly, many clients do not collect any data from their users. If your client does keep a customer database, you can analyze it (adhering to all privacy codes) to find their best customers. This database is only as good as the information it has captured, which is sometimes excellent, but not always. If your client will let you add questions to upcoming or ongoing current surveys, this is a quick, free way of getting more intel.

Let's assume the worst-case scenario: that their database is poor, they have no existing partnerships with tech or data companies who can help them, and they do not have any surveys onto which you can piggyback. In that case, you turn to subscription-based syndicated research—the traditional tools of media planners globally. Each syndicated brand owns a panel of over fifty thousand respondents who complete an annual survey that covers everything they see, do, buy, and believe, from the brands they prefer and the channels they favor, to what kind of person they feel they are. Two examples: "Others come to me for advice about electronics," or "I am a very stylish person."

This is a useful baseline tool. You simply input your client's brand (if the brand is big enough, it will be listed), and the tool spits out the demographics, behaviors, and preferences of its current users. What you are searching for is anyone who overindexes on each question, from a baseline of 100. Say, for example, you are thinking of including Pinterest in your media plan. When you look at women who actively use Pinterest, if a segment of women aged 55–65 underindexes at 86, versus the general population within the syndicated database, they are not a great target. But if women aged 25–35 overindex at 175, they are a significantly more viable target. By cross-tabulating data points, you can establish the best audience for a brand.

Media planners are generally the owners of syndicated and other media tools, but my team is extremely skilled at using these tools, too. Modern strategic planners need to be able to use every tool at their disposal, and in smaller agencies that subscribe to syndicated services but have no in-house media, the strategic planner often plays the role of communications planner. Either way, strategic planners need to understand their audiences' habits and behaviors as least as much as media planners do, so learning to use these tools is a must.

What if your agency, or client, does not subscribe to syndicated research, and your media partners cannot or will not allow you access? You can create a proprietary online survey to collect not only demographic, but also psychographic and behavioral data about existing customers. Your client can embed a link to the survey in an e-mail or SMS to their customers, put it on their social sites, incentivize it with a coupon, and with luck, enough people will complete it to give you a strong indication of their best customers.

You can also mine information from the brand's social media sites (again, adhering to all privacy laws). Incredibly useful information is available, via Facebook, in particular, including basic demographics, geography, their likes, their status, their preferences of brands, music, video, books, and hobbies. Facebook offers other useful tools, including an ad builder, which helps you find entire groups of people who fit within your target market. You can even jump into a conversation with them and ask specific questions about them and their relationship with your brand, or you can conduct polls among fans, as well as sharing links to surveys, as mentioned earlier.

Finally, what if none of this works? Your client has no useful data, you have no access to syndicated research, and the brand has few followers in social media (it happens). If you are working with a brand that is nonetheless quite popular, it is time to conduct your own primary quantitative research. To find users of obscure brands, it may be better to stick with qualitative research, such as online focus groups. Otherwise, your research vendor will have to reach deep into expensive consumer databases, and your survey will have to spend a long time in market as it struggles to screen out your audience. Deeper and longer equals more money.

FINDING PROSPECTIVE CUSTOMERS

Let's now assume that you have some great information about your current audience, and you are now looking to target prospects. To do this you use the demographic, psychographic, and behavioral facts that you learned about your existing audience to find a new audience that mirrors them, but is not yet buying your client's brand. To illustrate how this might work, let's pick an example.

If you are working with an upscale dairy client, you could use the syndicated tools to find people who enjoy cooking, are discerning, read high-end food magazines, stream food shows, and earn over $100,000 a year. The cross-tabs may indicate that the majority of these people are women aged 35–55 who are married or in a relationship, who have children, who are working full time, and who primarily live in the northeast.

This allows you to plan media around this specific target, so that the budget has the best chance of engaging the right audience. In this instance, you may plan to spend most of your $5 million in the Quad-State area and New England (avoiding Manhattan, which is *very* expensive), because you know your client has distribution there, but the brand isn't doing as well there as it is, say, in the Midwest. Because you know that your audience likes to watch upscale food programs, mostly on YouTube and other streaming services, you may dedicate the bulk of your spend to creating and producing a content series about cooking that you can air around their favorite shows. You may also know that your audience uses search to find recipes on a regular basis—so you place banners or rich media (digital ads with video, audio, or other interactive elements) in paid search or in their favorite recipe websites.

If syndicated isn't available to your agency (it is not free), you can also use some of the methodologies mentioned earlier, including engaging with your brand's social media fans and followers or by creating proprietary online surveys. Better still, if your client has captured data on lapsed or occasional customers, or, for example, those who abandoned baskets on their websites, or who downloaded a coupon but never used it. As well as retargeting those consumers to push them along, you can send a survey to them, along with an incentive, such as a coupon. Coupons are ideal, because not only will you get the research you need, but also your clients will benefit from encouraging a new group of customers to make a purchase and, hopefully, to engage with their brand.

LEARNING CUSTOMER SENTIMENT

When you have established who your target audience is, it's time to understand *what* they think of the category and the brand and *why* they think this.

Since you are potentially conducting some proprietary quantitative research to understand who your consumer is, in the same survey, you can ask questions about why they enter a category (the triggers), how they navigate it (the discovery process), and how they make decisions (the transaction). The benefit of quantitative research is, of course, scale, typically, on a national level. Most surveys have sample sizes of between at least one thousand and two thousand respondents, which can reassure you that the responses are consistent and likely representative of the broader target base. A larger sample size may reassure you and your clients, but it adds significant expense and it may not be necessary. In my experience, even at sample sizes of ten thousand-plus, the responses are not significantly different from those at a sample of two thousand.

Now, the downside of quantitative research is that while it can tell you *what* the consumers thinks and how they behave, unless you plant open-ended questions into the survey (and typically you can only add one or two before the respondent gets bored to death and exits the survey), it cannot tell you *why* they think and behave in this way. This can only be achieved through qualitative research.

I have gone into qualitative research in some detail in earlier chapters, so I will not overexpand on it here. Suffice to say, decide if ethnographies, shop-alongs, focus groups, online focus groups, one-on-ones, or another type of qualitative is best for your specific project. As mentioned before, I tend to favor ethnographies over traditional focus groups, because consumers are in the privacy of their personal space and thus more likely to be their authentic selves, rather than behaving formally or trying to lead or seek the approval of a group.

The corporate setting of a focus group facility doesn't always elicit more formal behavior. If the group isn't genuinely useful, it may at least provide you with stories that you will be telling friends and family for the rest of your lives. I have sat on the other side of the glass and witnessed respondents falling asleep in groups and actually snoring. I have seen many raise up their shirts to show the moderator their impressive scars. And on many occasions in the UK, typically, in the last groups of the day, I have seen people take advantage of the readily available alcoholic beverages on the drinks cart, to the point where they were slurring their words, becoming belligerent, or even keeling over mid-group. On one unforgettable occasion, a poor woman quickly tried to excuse herself from the group because she was feeling ill, didn't make it as far as the door, and projectile vomited over the one-way mirror—causing the large group of client observers to duck, somewhat unnecessarily. I once observed a focus group of older respondents discussing a new type of incontinence drug. When everyone had left the room, the poor facility manager had to scrub clean some of the chairs and blow-dry them with a hair-dryer in preparation for the next group. While mentioning this might sound mean spirited, I included it because it did give us a real sense of the severity of their condition, and the embarrassment it could cause when out in public. All good information.

Shop-alongs are always informative if you are working with a retail brand. Follow the respondent through the store and ask them to speak before, during, and after they shop, about the range of products they are considering and how they make selections. It's amazing how quickly people forget to be self-conscious and happily skip up the aisles, babbling loudly while you scurry to keep up. In this unguarded state, you will learn a consumer's true shopping habits. In a focus group environment, someone may try to impress their fellow respondents by saying they always buy the most expensive brand, but in the store you'll see them comparison shop and only buy leading brands if they are on sale. A demonstrated lack of brand loyalty is much more valuable and useful information. Remember to take notes, but unless you have advance permission from the store, do not film these outings, or you will soon feel the firm grip of a large hand on your shoulder.

Try to combine ethnographies with shop-alongs. Start in the respondent's home, go to the store with them, accompany them back to their home to observe them unload their groceries, and maybe even stay for dinner and see how they use the products and engage with their families. It's all good, honest insight. Do UX research by sitting down with respondents, after instructing them to, say, "spend fifty dollars on a new pair of jeans" and observing how they navigate different websites. Or ask them to give you permission to take over their screens, so that you can witness their behavior remotely.

Use whatever methodology works for you to get the best insights within the time allotted. At this point, a clear picture will be forming of the space your brand can uniquely occupy. This a very exciting point in the process. You're almost at the brief and briefing stage—all that is left to do now is to analyze your brand.

Brand Analysis

Brand analysis is essentially a brand health check: an opportunity to pull apart and examine all of your brand assets and elements. If a brand is a promise made and kept with consumers or customers, then it is important to determine the state of that relationship (and prospective relationships).

Start by determining what kind of brand you have. Use the brand family tool in Chapter 3 to see if your brand is an Alpha, Youth, Newborn, or Old Dog. Learn about how your brand ended up in the space it occupies now. What happened? What didn't happen? What needs to happen? Establish where you are now and where you need to be to succeed. Typically, that will involve moving from:

- Newborn to Youth
- Youth to Alpha
- Old Dog to Alpha (or, in some cases, Youth)

Now use your research to create one or two perception maps to establish how current customers and prospects feel about the brand and what they associate it with. (You can add these questions to any quantitative surveys going into the field for your consumer analysis.) For example, if you have chosen to map brands against adjectives, and your brand is considered brave, forward thinking, innovative, progressive, and modern, then all is well. If you are considered old-fashioned, tired, conservative, slow, or lazy, then it is time for some serious brand repositioning. If they feel that your brand is a lion, you are in good shape. If they feel your brand is a tortoise, not so much.

After establishing what kind of brand you are, what you need to be, and how you might get there, it is time to examine your current brand assets. These include:

brand heritage—Why does your brand exist? Who created it and why? Is the heritage well-known, but holding the brand back? Or is it dormant and unknown, but very relevant today?

Remember Fred the Baker? Because Dunkin' Donuts' focus was on beverages, and Fred was associated with donuts, it was time to leave him and his "Time to make the donuts" line behind. It can be hard to walk away from a strong brand heritage; consumers grow sentimental about certain brand assets and will often beg you not to change anything. But sentimentality does not make the cash registers ring. If consumers are not engaging, and the brand is entering Old Dog territory, it's time to move on. Time to evolve.

The opposite can also happen. When I first started working with the Chili's brand, it was a generic casual dining brand with no known heritage, indistinguishable from many others in the crowded category. In stakeholder interviews—including one with a Chili's founder—we were astonished to learn that Chili's had been created in the 1970s by a group of hippie bikers who, quite simply, loved chili. They opened their first Chili's shack in Dallas, and the brand soon took off. Over the years, this heritage had been lost, and the brand had become generic.

Younger Millennials and Gen Zers, who seek authentic brands with a strong sense of self and shared values, did not know this story and were not dining at Chili's. So, we created a campaign that introduced the brand heritage with grainy footage reminiscent of the 1970s shack and the original founders. We found in our research that younger generations were pleasantly surprised to learn about Chili's past, as were their core users, who had been equally clueless.

Knowing the brand had a strong, authentic provenance allowed customers to form a sense of pride and allegiance to Chili's.

visual identity—These assets include the logo, typeface, visual style, colors, and design elements. Look at each visual asset. Check the home page and the rest of their website. Look at any other brand design elements, from brochures to white papers, annual reports, and social media presence.

Look at the history of the brand's logo and color palette. Is the logo dated? If so, would the client consider a new or refreshed logo? A word of caution here: before you go telling a client their logo needs to be updated, consider the cost of such an exercise. A logo change entails renovated physical storefronts and other expensive changes. A new logo can take years to roll out, and such a dramatic shift is not always possible. Also, do your homework: check to see if your client went through this exercise recently. They do not want to hear you recommend a revamp when they made a big change just 2 years before. However, if the logo or colors are seriously outdated, and this is affecting brand perception and hindering progress, it is worth mentioning, even as a potential, longer-term objective, so also make that a consideration.

brand beliefs—Is anything the consumer believes about your brand holding you back? Assess the health of brand beliefs and the reasons behind them. You will have learned much from your brand perception maps and other research. Is the brand perceived negatively at all? Did the brand experience any recent scandal affecting its reputation? A severely damaged reputation can be fixed, but it takes time to ensure it can never fall into that dark space again and demands that the brand prove it has changed beyond every measure. It can take decades for a brand to recover from a corporate scandal. Consumers have very long memories. In rare cases, these perceptions are passed down from one generation to the next, and the brand never recovers.

Consumer memory can work in a brand's favor, too. Do older consumers know something positive about your brand that younger consumers do not, but that would resonate? For example, working with the American Red Cross (ARC) we learned that while the ARC was associated with blood drives, fundraising, and of course emergency assistance, it touches many American families in everyday ways, including teaching kids at local pools how to swim and educating families about emergency preparedness. But because the ARC was associated with "disaster relief," many research respondents did not feel as personally connected with it as they might. Learning about ARC's involvement in their own communities gave them a sense of personal affinity with and ownership of the brand, which made more people more likely to give time or blood, or make a donation to the ARC.

Internal Audience

There is one critical audience that is all too frequently overlooked. A brand house, or even just a new brand purpose or tagline, will not succeed if there is not buy-in from the internal audience: employees.

Few employees beyond the marketing department will know how to reposition a brand, but they will know how they feel about the work you share with them, whether they are inspired and excited, neutral, or not on board at all. Even if you believe it is the best work of your career, it will not flourish unless most employees believe in it. About 70–80 percent is enough for buy-in, especially if that number includes the culture keepers and influencers of the company. There will always be naysayers, and that's okay—stay realistic and don't be discouraged. You are looking for a majority vote to get things moving.

Engaging employees is tricky. You want them to help inform and inspire your new brand house or campaign idea, but you do not want to seek their approval at every stage of the process. For example, you definitely do not need or want their help in choosing positioning statements, or taglines. Some of the best taglines of all time probably sounded clunky or weird to employees on first exposure. Think about "Drivers wanted" for Volkswagen (VW), which was created by the legendary Lance Jensen and his team. This line would only have made sense to the extended employee base when it was paired with the ramp line: "On the road of life there are passengers and there are drivers. Drivers wanted."

Employees do need to feel they have been involved, however. If they have influenced the work in some way, shape, or form, they will see their thumbprints in it, even if only in a small way, and they will be much more likely to buy in. When employees buy in, they will become the brand's biggest advocates and champions.

The best way to involve them is to include as many as possible in your 1:1 stakeholder interviews at the beginning of the process. For the remaining (majority) of employees, a survey works well, again, early on in the process. Work with your client's HR department (HR folks can understandably get prickly about this kind of stuff if they are not included or co-leading) to create and launch a custom survey. Ask employees questions such as:

· What makes you proud to work here?

· What makes you frustrated about working here?

· How do you describe to other people what we do?

· Why do you believe this company (or brand) exists?

· How would you describe our culture?

· What do you like most about our culture?

· What do you like the least?

· How do you feel about our recent merger/acquisition?

· How, if at all, has it changed our culture, for better or worse?

· What do you think of our current logo/ad campaign/corporate colors?

The responses will provide much incredibly valuable information that can influence many decisions. You and your team will constantly ask yourselves, "Will the employees feel proud to be associated with a company that stands for this, based on what I know about them?" Or, "Does this campaign reflect the best of the culture of the brand now or where it needs to go?"

When the brand house or campaign idea is complete, roll it out to employees *first*, at a company-wide meeting (or a fun, virtual meeting). Find creative ways of sharing content and ideas with them. Branded swag is always appreciated. As analogue as it may seem, there is no better way to get the message out there than having ten thousand employees wearing a T-shirt with the brand's new tagline and logo on it, or having them share that great new content on their personal social media sites. More importantly, a brand purpose and/or new tagline gives employees something to rally around. It becomes an important "war cry" for the entire company, from CEO to janitor. It provides that all-important North Star for the whole organization.

YOU HAVE DONE A LOT, but there is still work to be done. If your client doesn't have a brand house, or at least a brand purpose, vision, or positioning, you will now be informed enough to help them create one using the brand house workshop guidelines in Chapter 4. Before the workshop, share all of your learning to date with the extended team. Hopefully, you and your client will have been in lockstep throughout the discovery process, but there will be many more client and agency team members who will benefit from the knowledge you now have, so include them at this stage.

When everyone is equally informed, it is time to let the rubber hit the road. Time to develop a campaign for your client that brings all of these new assets to their consumers and prospects, as well as their internal audience. All of that starts with the most important document that any strategic planner has ever owned and will ever own: the creative brief.

seven

The Creative
Brief

T
HE CREATIVE BRIEF is not a sacred text. But it is the clos-
est thing to it that a planner will create. As legendary creative
director Dave Trott, whom I was privileged enough to work
with earlier in my career, wrote in his book *Creative Mischief*, "The
brief was always supposed to be a springboard for great work. Not a
straitjacket."

What is it? Well, it's "exactly what it says on the tin" (in case you
didn't catch it, this is my homage to Dave Trott, who created that
famous tagline for Ronseal)—it's a *brief* for *creatives*. The brief is the
final document that summarizes everything you have learned about
culture, the consumer, the category, and the brand, including the
consumer research you fielded. You may have heard the phrase "crap
in, crap out"? That still applies. As does the reverse: "greatness in,
greatness out."

Today, "the brief" is in fact a suite of briefs. There is the main
campaign (or brand) brief that everyone will use as the blueprint

for new strategic or creative directions. There is also the extension brief, a much shorter version of the main brief that includes only the basic needs of the assignment. This type of brief is typically used when adding ideas to an existing campaign. For example, for Dunkin' Donuts, an extension brief might be used to introduce a new seasonal coffee flavor. There are other specialized briefs, including content briefs, digital briefs, and media briefs, which include technical details for the creatives, technologists, producers, and media planners and buyers. All of these are secondary to the main brief. They inform assignments that are extensions of something bigger. Even something as small as a single banner or social post has to come from the same voice, so that the brand experience for the consumer remains consistent.

The main campaign brief is the blueprint for every brief that surrounds it. Over the decades agencies have tried to make this document as complicated as possible. We went from the one-page or even one-word (or in the case of one London agency, the nonexistent) brief early on in my career, to a multipage brief a few years ago, when digital and social were brought into the mix.

After trying every possible format and style of brief, I have landed right back at the beginning: the one-page brief. My team's brief template even says at the foot of the page, "If your brief is running onto a second page it is too long." If the brief is longer than one page, I reject it and expect the creatives to do the same. Why? Because a planner who cannot write a short brief is a lazy thinker. And, after all, it is called the "brief" for a reason. A message has only a few seconds to engage the consumer. Regardless of the channel, the work needs to pull them in quickly. To do that it must be short, pithy, and engaging. The brief that inspires the work needs to be equally short and pithy.

The brief should not be a checklist of everything your client wants the campaign idea to spell out. When creative teams receive a brief that is too long, or inconsistent, scattered with different pieces of information that don't form a coherent story, they will cherry-pick the juiciest pieces to focus on and do whatever they feel like doing. Those may be the least important parts of the whole brief. A good brief focuses on what is most important, most relevant, and most motivating and simplifies everything into one short, compelling story.

Here are the basic principles of getting to a great brief:

- The brief is a compelling, concise statement informed by everything you have learned about what the advertising needs to do to move the brand forward.

- The rest of the team should give input, but the planner is responsible for writing the brief—they will decide what to include and what to omit.

- The brief is not a sausage to be stuffed with as many ingredients as possible until it splits apart—it needs to hold together.

- The language should be simple and clear—every creative person, including the least experienced members, needs to understand it perfectly.

- The brief needs to inspire, not dictate.

- The brief should tell a story from start to finish—the climax is "the single most important idea" section. This is where the creatives will focus their energy—so, spend most of your time on it.

- The brief needs to be one page long—anything longer equals lazy thinking.

- If a word isn't essential, eliminate it—less is more.

- Share the first draft with creatives, so they can let you know if it will be workable or not. If they come up with a better idea for any part of the brief, and it is in line with the agreed-upon audience and strategic direction, incorporate it. There is no pride of ownership here. The consumer will never know who wrote the brief, nor would they ever care. Success for you will be the amazing work that comes from your good brief. That's all that matters.

- The briefing is as important as the brief (more on that later).

The Brief

A typical campaign brief template of mine looks like the example below. Most agencies have something similar to this, though some choose to make things more complicated. There is absolutely no need for that. The simpler and more concise the brief template, the simpler and more concise the brief, and the better the work.

ASSIGNMENT:

DATE WRITTEN:

FIRST REVIEW:

AUTHOR:

What is the business problem?

What will success look like?

Who are we talking to?

What do they currently think about us?

What do we want them to think?

What action do we want them to take?

What single idea will get us there?

What are the reasons to believe this?

What is our personality?

What are the known deliverables and mandates?

The best way for me to illustrate how you get to a good brief is to share an example with you. So here goes. Let's pick the Chili's campaign I mentioned earlier.

WHAT IS THE BUSINESS PROBLEM?

I deliberately and consciously use the words "business problem" instead of "marketing or advertising problem." The whole agency team needs to understand exactly what the campaign is trying to do. They need to understand the needle they are trying to move, even in its simplest terms. It's not enough to say that the campaign needs to "raise awareness" or "build brand predisposition." These things may be true, and you can include them in the brief, but the business problem outlines specific KPIs of success.

For example, are we trying to expand our customer base, because our current customer is aging out of the category? If so, by what percentage year over year (YOY)? What percentage will start to reverse that trend? Why did this happen in the first place? Or, are we trying to steal share in a crowded category? Who is the leader, and who stole share from us? How did that happen? What percentage share can we reasonably expect to steal back, based on our media weight versus the competition and past performance metrics?

In the case of Chili's, the brand team understood the business problem very well.

Response: There is little differentiation between Chili's and its competitors. The category as a whole has suffered a decline in traffic of 1.8 percent on average over the last 13 weeks. Chili's traffic is declining faster than the category, at an average of 3 percent nationally, over the last 13 weeks.*

---

* While the outline of the case study is true, all figures relating to Chili's are fictional, invented for the purpose of this exercise.

WHAT WILL SUCCESS LOOK LIKE?

What will fix the problem? Again, from a *business* perspective. The fix has to be reasonable, based on media weight versus the competition, past performance data, and, importantly, the latest news.

In the case of Chili's, the traffic goals had been carefully calculated, based on past media and performance data. The goal was reasonable in light of the decline in traffic Chili's experienced, and there were no other variables at play, such as seasonality. Plus, Chili's was launching two new burger choices to feature in the campaign, which would help create news.

Response: Increase Chili's traffic by 3.5 percent nationally over the next 16 weeks.

WHO ARE WE TALKING TO?

This is your opportunity to refine the audience you chose during customer analysis. Avoid the common sin of making the target age range too broad: many clients, fearful of missing out, request we target "adults aged 18–55." First, maybe it's because I'm getting older, but I believe that it is shortsighted to cut off the target age at 55, when those aged 56 and older cover two generations and in some instances three. Those in their 50s and 60s today represent Gen X and second-wave boomers. For context, that means they were teenagers when Led Zeppelin, Jimi Hendrix, Prince, Sex Pistols, and Joy Division were at their peak—those are very different formative influences. They are also the wealthiest cohorts at present, which makes them lucrative targets. (I'm not suggesting you extend the age range in this example, but you get the point about older segments that I am trying to make.) Second, a campaign that appeals to an 18-year-old would possibly turn off a 30-year-old, never mind a 55-year-old. Insist to the client that you focus on a core target covering no more than a 10-year range. If younger and older audiences overhear your message, that's fine, but trying to appeal to everyone will weaken the point of view, strip out the cultural relevance, and have no desired effect.

In the case of Chili's, which has excellent customer data, we learned the audience comprised two parts: first-wave (older) Millennial families primarily, and empty nester boomer couples secondarily. There was a gap in between where Gen Xers were not going to Chili's as much as they used to, and second-wave Millennials and Generation Z were not going at all (apart from in some regions, where choice was severely limited). This data confirmed the issue: the audience was getting older and moving away from the brand as their children aged, so Gen Zers and second-wave Millennials were critical to the future success of the brand. They would be the focus of our advertising. Gen X would overhear these messages and be reminded of why they had once loved Chili's, hopefully encouraging them to return, as couples or with their older children.

This stage is also the time to add color and texture to your audience—the psychographics. From our cultural analysis and qualitative research, we knew that our target cohorts loved authentic brands. They favored brands with a strong provenance and sought out brand experiences that were true to the brand's heritage. Like most cohorts, while they craved variety and excitement, they were deeply overwhelmed by school, work, and the fast pace of life. They were heavy users of social media and streaming video, but their addiction to technology made them yearn, at least on occasion, for a simpler life and a simpler time. They enjoyed movies and shows that portrayed this, especially those from the 1970s and 1980s such as the original *Star Trek* series, *Star Wars*, and the *Breakfast Club*/Brat Pack movies. They also enjoyed music from the 1970s and 1980s, Southern rock, and Coachella-type fashion.

Response: The primary audience is culturally and ethnically diverse 18-30-year-olds, who will bring new energy to the Chili's brand and will influence older Gen X audiences. They are a mainstream audience who works hard and long hours, but their tastes are far from mainstream. They love authenticity and respect brands that are true to who they are, while disliking brands that feel forced or pretentious, or have no point of view. They constantly seek new experiences in music, movies, stores, and brands. This also extends to restaurants, which they choose on impulse. They are heavy users of social media and are influenced by video.

WHAT DO THEY CURRENTLY THINK ABOUT US?

This is where you summarize what consumers told you they feel about the brand during the research process. Does the consumer have an opinion? Is it positive or negative? Have they heard of the brand (awareness) but may not be familiar with it?

Our research for Chili's told us that nationally the audience was almost 100 percent aware of the brand in terms of aided recall (when respondents were asked if they had heard of Chili's). Unaided recall (when respondents were asked to identify brands in the casual dining space, without brand names being revealed) was exceptionally high, too. Familiarity scores were weak (meaning, there was a lot of misconception or lack of knowledge of the brand). Most respondents assumed the brand was for families with kids, not for them. Many also held the misconception that the brand sold Americanized Mexican food (the name didn't help), whereas they preferred to visit authentic Mexican restaurants, instead.

Response: "I know Chili's, but isn't it just generic Tex-Mex food? Isn't it for families, not couples or groups of friends? I have no idea why they might be different from the other boring, bland casual dining restaurants in my area."

WHAT DO WE WANT THEM TO THINK?

Having identified the brand's unique features and your audience's wants and needs, this is when you determine how to move the brand from one place to another—in this case, borderline Old Dog status to Alpha status—resulting in a positive outcome.

We knew that Chili's was the only true brand in the casual dining space with a strong and relevant heritage. We also knew how important this was to our target audience, so this was a great opportunity to connect the dots.

Response: Chili's is an authentic Texan restaurant from the 1970s with an exciting, crave-worthy menu of delicious food with kicked-up flavors. It is the opposite of boring and bland—distinct from and better than other casual dining restaurants.

WHAT ACTION DO WE WANT THEM TO TAKE?

KPIs can only be achieved if the consumer takes action. It is not enough to state that the consumer should "consider" a brand. They need to actually do something that benefits the brand. Depending on what success looks like for the client, that can range from clicking on a banner or video content or buying a product online, to buying a skin-care brand from a pharmacy or walking into a restaurant, instead of driving right on by.

Response: Whether alone or with friends or family, the next time they feel like eating out, they will go directly to Chili's.

WHAT SINGLE IDEA WILL GET US THERE?

This is the central focus and the most important sentence on the brief. It is also the hardest part to write and, aside from the "business problem," the part I am most likely to challenge. Typically, this is because:

- It is far too long or complicated.
- There is more than one idea in the "single idea."
- It includes punctuation, such as a comma or semicolon (it cannot be a single idea if it includes punctuation).
- It's boring or uninspiring.
- It's generic.

Writing a strong single idea requires getting the balance right. Many creatives like you to push against a nemesis, which can be a category, a competitor, a feeling, or a behavior. In this case, Chili's pushed against the generic, the inauthentic, and the fake, which was effective, because of its authentic roots, and the real, fresh ingredients Chili's prides itself in using; it was the only brand in the category that could plausibly do this.

Response: Get real at Chili's.

WHAT ARE THE REASONS TO BELIEVE THIS?

The most common sin in this section is to add everything you couldn't fit into the rest of the brief, so that the client checklist is completed. Do not do this. Select the two or three reasons to believe (RTBs) that best support the single idea and eliminate the rest. It's okay to add a link to background information on the brand, but even that should be simple and factual. Don't force the creatives to dig around, looking for insight in different places. The brief should be enough.

Response: Real? In 1975, people in Dallas stood in a line that wrapped around the corner of Greenville Avenue and Meadow Road. They were waiting to sample the delicious food and casual atmosphere of a funky, new burger joint called Chili's that some Harley-riding hippies had opened. Chili's has always been kicked up, right from the start. Their famous baby back ribs are triple basted with Chili's own barbecue sauce and fall right off the bone. Or try their tantalizing, sizzling fajitas and mouth-watering, napkin-soaking, grilled gourmet burgers. There has never been anything generic about this food or this place. No, sir.

WHAT IS OUR PERSONALITY?

If your brand were a person, how would you describe them, in three words or fewer? Again, don't use this section to add to the client checklist; instead, really think about the brand's best character traits, as well as those that need to be ramped up, so as to leave wiggle room for the future.

Chili's had a strong personality—as a fun-loving, authentic brand, where everything was dialed up a notch—but it was only known by employees and brand loyalists.

Response: Spirited. Fun. Genuine.

WHAT ARE THE KNOWN DELIVERABLES AND MANDATES?

I have approved briefs with no mandatories, only to learn at the client presentation, after 4 weeks of creative ideation, that the tagline could absolutely not change, or the brand mascot had to be included in the idea. This is such a profound waste of time. Do *not* be fearful of creatives whining when they learn that the brand mascot needs to be in the work—if it's mandatory, put it in the brief and accept the barrage of expletives that will no doubt ensue. That is far preferable to letting them bust a gut writing ideas that exclude the mascot and then having to tell them the client rejected the work. Creatives will likely hear about any mandatories at the same time as the planner or account team, but sometimes it slips through the net. Don't let that happen.

Response: Use existing logo. Feature new burgers.

THE CAMPAIGN THAT came from this brief was the retro video and digital campaign I mentioned earlier, featuring a fantastic 1970s rock soundtrack and the tagline "Chili's. Chillin' since 1975." Because the brief was concise, it did most of the heavy lifting, freeing the creatives to focus on what they do best (instead of searching for an interesting theme in a long, complicated brief). Happily, the campaign reversed the traffic decline and pulled in younger Millennials and Gen Zers, proving that when you do your homework, you'll write a good brief that leads to relevant work that works.

The Briefing

The creative briefing is as important as the creative brief. Early in my career, I worked at an agency where the chief strategy officer banned paper briefs, believing this would ensure good in-person briefings. It's not a terrible idea.

Briefing is a dying art that badly needs to be revitalized. Today's agencies are so time crunched that it is all too tempting to skip the briefing and just e-mail the brief to the creatives. Never, ever just e-mail a brief. And never do what I did all those years ago with my very first brief, when I literally tossed it into the hands of the creatives and stepped back, waiting for either applause or hateful rejection.

The point of the briefing is to take the creatives through the story of the brand and the brief in as compelling a way as possible. The final written brief should not come as a big surprise to anyone, since you engaged creatives and other team members in the first draft. But it is still your job as the planner to make the briefing as engaging, interesting, and even as fun as possible. Take the time to prepare for it properly, without cutting corners, so that the team can experience the brand.

It is also an opportunity for the creatives to ask questions or seek clarity. For example, if you have worked on a complex business for some time, but this is your creative team's first assignment, your knowledge is significantly ahead of theirs. It helps to simplify it as much as possible. I once worked with a client who was in an incredibly complex medical technology space that was almost impossible to understand. Our chief creative officer (CCO) was having trouble wrapping his head around it, probably because I wasn't doing a good job explaining it to him. It wasn't my job to teach him everything I knew about their business. It was my job to simplify it and explain it the way I would to a customer or consumer. The consumer doesn't need to understand the complexities of medical technology. They just need to understand the basic principles and how it helps make the system better, to help them—ultimately, this is what a consumer cares about.

After mulling over this dilemma, I decided the best way for me to explain the complex nature of the technology and what this brand actually did was to describe it to the CCO this way: "You know the plastic that holds a six-pack together? Well, that is what they do. They hold it all together."

Enough said. He got it.

When choosing a location for the briefing, context is everything. Invite the extended creative team (digital, traditional, social, content, etc.) to join you in a casual space outside their offices. Creatives are busy people, as are you, so don't ask them to walk or take a cab for an hour, and neutral ground is best. If there is a relevant outside location that would help the briefing be successful, go for it, but keep it close.

If you are promoting a car, rent a car and take a drive together. If you are advertising a product like packaged cheese (what is it with me and cheese?), then bring some to the agency and share it, along with some good bread and wine. What if you are assigned to a hemorrhoids product? Well, at the very least have the product at hand for the briefing. Just do what it takes to make the brief come to life. It will pay off.

I was once creating a brief for a new campaign for a famous dog food. To my disadvantage, neither of the creatives I was working with had ever owned a dog, and so I was having a challenging time explaining to them not only the strength of the relationship between owner and dog, but also the common bond among dog owners themselves. I postponed the briefing for 24 hours and got clearance from my building to bring my high-energy boxer puppy to work the next day. The creative teams' jaws dropped with surprise, as I pushed Biff into their office and gently closed the door. I yelled through the crack that they should "take him for a walk around Green Park and then you will get it." They were gone for a worryingly long time. And on their return, they confessed that my cute puppy had attracted a lot of attention from some nice young women, with whom they had enjoyed conversing very much. But they did finally "get it."

AT THIS POINT, you should have a more robust understanding of the process of planning advertising, and the role a strategist plays in developing great, effective work. You will also have learned that strategic planning has transformed significantly as a discipline since its birth in the 1960s, to the point of being barely recognizable. Yes, the work is the most important thing an agency can offer. However, research and data both play an incredibly important role in modern strategic planning. As fantastic and necessary as this all is, the feather in each Super Strategist's cap is the customer journey.

eight
The Customer Journey

E VERY DAY THE very definition of creative evolves. The role of
an agency today is not just to make ads—we also create brand
experiences that help the customer navigate a path through
the customer journey, to ultimately stick with, buy, or try a product
or service.

Just as every consumer touchpoint is "brand" today, and every
potential messaging platform is "media," the same applies to "creative." What was once confined to TV, print, radio, and outdoor can
now be any living surface—any auditory, olfactory, or tactile experience you can imagine. It's all brand. It's all media. It's all creative.

Creative could mean a billboard to induce predisposition towards
a brand. It may mean a long-form video to create familiarity and consideration. It may mean an app that helps the customer compare your
brand to others. It may be the customer's experience of a changing
room, or a car dealership or a grocery store, or the smell of a fashion
retailer. It may be the addition of a tasting room, or a fantastic, flat-
tering mirror, or a digital map to help consumers navigate the store.
Each of these creative solutions helps pull the customer through the

journey by solving problems, creating delightful experiences, and, ultimately, creating loyalty.

This chapter outlines how the strategic planner spearheads the entire process of journey development. (For a sneak peek at a completed version, see page 163.) This is the most significant and important of all their tools, where each and every element of their expertise comes together to serve the fundamental goals.

Why Do You Need a Customer Journey in the First Place?

Customer journey mapping is critical to help us understand where the customer starts, where they lose interest, where we can pull them back in again. Where the product, online, or in-store experience succeeds or fails. And where the belief that the brand delivers against its purpose succeeds or fails. And, ultimately, how shareable that experience is—for better or for worse.

While syndicated research can provide us with a lot of useful information about our consumers, their lifestyles, attitudes, and media consumption, it has its limitations. Syndicated is survey based, and therefore it relies upon consumer belief and intention that is not always reflective of actual behavior. Adding a customer journey to the mix provides an extra layer of accuracy to planning media. It also does so, so much more.

I have mentioned how the traditional purchase funnel or loyalty loop are now outdated. The consumer meanders through the decision-making process, falling in and out of the journey, adding and subtracting brands all along the way, changing behavior and attitudes in response to different inputs. A customer journey map is the most accurate reflection of how those decisions are made. It helps us perceive their emotions—the highs and lows along the way—thus helping us understand the best medium and message to keep them engaged until they make a purchase.

It not only highlights advertising opportunities, but it also frequently finds business opportunities. For example, while doing customer journey work for Planet Fitness, we learned (through proprietary research) that a surprising number of first-time visitors to the gym sit in the parking lot, fearful of entering the building, then turn right around and go home. Why? Because many first timers are older and/or out of shape. They are self-conscious and shy, and they know that the first thing they will see when they open the door is a young, fit person greeting them. They told us that this is extremely intimidating. Talking about their fitness goals in front of other members is also terrifying. We suggested that staff immediately take new members to a separate room to discuss their reasons for joining the gym and recommend a plan—and to have a box of tissues nearby, because this can be an emotional process. This had nothing to do with advertising and everything to do with human insight resulting in a business opportunity.

It's important to explain the benefits of journey work to clients. Most clients love customer journey workshops, but some are dragged to them kicking and screaming, opining, "Why do we need to spend a whole day teaching you about our business?" The primary point of these workshops is not to learn about a client's business (although that is a helpful side benefit) but rather, it is to learn about opportunities and threats throughout the journey that may be getting in the way of success and that could be resolved in many different ways. In my decade of developing journeys, I have *never* met a client who did not learn something new and critical from this work, such as a flaw in customer service or an obvious issue with their website.

Frequently, clients who focus on a singular point of customer contact—for example, social platforms, the website, or call centers—have no idea how consumers, or even money, moves through the rest of the journey beyond their small corner of it. Understanding the *entire journey*, and the cracks and flaws that inevitably exist along the way, is extremely important to everyone who touches the brand. Each crack spiders outward, to be felt by every customer at some point. Cracks result in money left on the table—a thought that is typically quite motivating to clients.

TO ILLUSTRATE THE process of customer journey development, let's pick a category and an imaginary brand—one that allows us to touch on real-life opportunities and threats I have encountered with other brands—and then go through the steps that I have outlined in previous chapters. This is the best way to demonstrate each and every piece of the strategic planners' tool kit in action. Let's use our imaginary brand journey (but I will refer to personal consumer and category knowledge) to establish how a consumer may stick to the brand throughout their path to purchase.

Let's imagine you have a financial services client with a brand called, say, Newbury Bank. They are a family-owned bank with two thousand-plus branches in the Eastern U.S., mostly (30 percent) in the northeast, where their first branch opened almost 100 years ago. The bank provides consumer bank services, including checking and savings accounts, as well as mortgages and loans. In addition, Newbury has three hundred in-branch financial advisors, who help mass affluent consumers with retirement planning and other investments. The bank does not sell any other financial products, like CDs. The bank's current CEO is the eldest daughter of the previous CEO. The role has been passed down from parent to child, over each generation. The bank has not significantly invested in communications (beyond local ads and branch-opening PR) for the last 8 years, instead relying mostly on word of mouth.

What Is the Business Problem?

Remember, the *business* problem is just that. Not a marketing problem. Not an advertising problem. It is the specific business metric that the identification and repair of weak spots in the journey will address. For example, the business problem could be a sudden loss of share. Or the company was bought by a larger bank, and employees are shaken and confused. Or the company's sales have declined YOY for the last 5 years. Work with your clients to clearly identify the issue you are trying to solve.

In practice, the journey sometimes informs the business problem, or they develop in tandem. The journey always provides value, but sometimes the client doesn't know the issue, and the journey helps to establish it.

In this case, let's assume the following:

Newbury Bank has 450 branches in the southeast. However, these branches significantly underperform, compared to a similar number of branches in the northeast, and that number has been steadily declining by around 8 percent YOY over the last 5 years.

What Are Your Objectives?

Next, you need to establish with your client what specifically the journey is trying to achieve. Is it needed to teach the sales force how to spot and fill in leaks in the sales process? Is it to teach HR how each prospective employee navigates job searches? Or is it for the whole sales and marketing team to fully understand how the customer makes decisions, and where the holes and opportunities are to reinforce their brand experience? The answer will determine which particular journey you are going to focus on. There are, of course, many journey paths to follow; one customer journey will probably not be enough for any given brand, because there are so many brand questions that need answers, such as:

· How does the customer enter a category and choose a brand, including ours?

· How does a particular demographic segment experience our brand, compared to the general population?

· How can current customers' brand experience help us grow our business organically?

· Why are current customers moving away from our brand online and in-store?

· What is our employees' experience of working at the company, from the first recruitment ad to their exit interview?

A good way of summing up the objective of the work is to write a "problem statement." The whole team can rally around this and refer back to it to ensure that as the work evolves, you do not lose track of what you are trying to achieve.

So the problem statement for Newbury Bank could be something like this:

> While successful in the northeast, Newbury Bank is underperforming in the southeast. We need to understand the problem for Newbury Bank in the southeast, so that we can reverse the trend and help the brand grow again, while setting the precedent for successful future branch openings in that region.

Choose Your Team

When you have agreed upon what the journey will be used for, then it is time to assemble your team. You need to pick your team carefully. This is not a solo endeavor. As the strategic planner you will lead journey development, but it is important to involve key people throughout. From the agency side, your core account, creative, and media leads will typically be involved, and from the client side, key members of the marketing and sales teams, plus any other people, such as other agency partners, who you feel will be critical to the creation of an accurate journey story.

What Is Your Plan?

Let's assume the client doesn't have any of the data in hand that would be needed for their growth objective to succeed. Also, customer data for all financial services is, reassuringly, highly regulated, so access would be impossible. Research will be needed, but it alone would not be enough. Huge decisions and investments will be made based on this work, so the recommendations have to be as watertight as possible. For the team to puzzle out what is going wrong in the southeast and repair the cracks, they will also need to do a complete analysis, culminating in the development of the customer journey.

What Are the KPIs of Success?

Work with your clients, their data analysts, or with your own in-house data analysts and business strategists to establish how many new accounts need to be opened and how to optimize organic growth (or prevent churn). Establish reasonable timelines and a budget to help achieve these goals.

Let's assume you have done all the necessary work (see "The KPIs of Success," page 94, in Chapter 6) and established the following goal:

> Increase the annual number of new accounts opened in the southeast by 25 percent over the next 12 months. Encourage organic growth by actively connecting 5 percent of existing customers with a Newbury financial advisor to help them create an investment and retirement plan, within the next 12 months, on a budget of approximately $5 million, including production.

Category Analysis

To start, carefully study the key dynamics of the rapidly evolving financial services category. There is a lot of secondary research out there that can teach you about the category quickly (see "Competitive Analysis," page 102, in Chapter 6).

Another great way to get smart fast is to hire a category expert and pick their brain for an hour or two. In this case it could be a former executive from the bank, or a university professor with profound knowledge of the industry. Or, if you have little or no budget, it's amazing what an all-staff e-mail can do. Many employees will have industry contacts or family members in the sector, and they may be willing to talk to you for no fee, just to help out their friend or family member.

What you will learn is that the most dynamic shift in the category is, of course, the evolution of fintech—non-traditional mobile-first financial offerings such as PayPal, Zelle, and Venmo in the U.S.; popular online banks, such as Monzo and Revolut in the United Kingdom; and established technology companies that deliver financial products as part of a broader service offering, such as Amazon and Apple.

In the context of fintech, Newbury Bank has to consider certain key products as table stakes. An outstanding mobile banking experience and competitive products, for example, are prerequisites to be in the category. Newbury also has to consider why anyone would choose them over fintech. Finally, the bank needs to consider what makes it different from other, similar community-based national brands.

Well, it's a family-owned, community-based bank, and it has financial advisors in hundreds of its branches, who can advise people one-on-one, in person, or by phone, on a variety of subjects, including navigating a career change, investing in a college savings plan, or preparing for a life change, such as a relocation. Fintech cannot do this. Smaller, regional banks do not have advisors or the breadth of products that a brand of Newbury Bank's size may have, while huge national or global banks cannot offer the same degree of intimacy. Newbury Bank is the right scale and size to offer the consumer the best of both worlds.

Brand Analysis

To begin this stage, organize stakeholder interviews at the bank. The internal audience is vital. Ask to speak with 10–15 key people across different disciplines who can tell you about the bank's current strengths, weaknesses, opportunities, and threats; its heritage; and how they believe the brand needs to evolve. This is foundational work that will establish where the brand is now and how it needs to change to succeed. These interviews will also teach you how employees feel about the bank's culture and values, and how it feels to work for the bank. If your client's HR department hasn't given you recent employee data (and if you have the time), it is also worth surveying a broader spectrum of employees.

With your category and brand research in hand, conduct the "brand family" exercise (see Chapter 3). You know that Newbury Bank is 100 years old and well established in the northeast (NE), but not in the southeast (SE) and other parts of the country. Therefore, it has a complex brand family status. In the NE, it is an Alpha brand, the leader in the region—but at some point in the future, the brand may be in danger of slipping into the Old Dog segment, if there is a lack of ongoing investment in the brand. In the SE, where most branches were established only 10–20 years ago, it is a Youth brand. Plans for national expansion are on hold until the health of the southeastern region improves. Brand bifurcation—when the brand is in different life stages across regions—is not unusual for franchise or service industries, where the brand is stronger in its region of origin, and weaker in areas that the brand has more recently expanded into.

At some point, investment may be required to help retain Newbury Bank's Alpha status in the northeast. For now, the brand is still healthy in that region, but the $5 million budget for all communications for the year is not as much as it sounds, given the high cost of media and production. Focus is, therefore, key. With a limited budget, it is better to focus on one specific target in a smaller number of locations with one key objective. If the spend is spread too thin nationally, not enough people will hear the message to make a difference. Therefore, because the brand has stable growth in the northeast, with no customer retention issues, the smartest decision for Newbury Bank would be to develop a campaign idea, using paid media, and focus on attracting new audiences in the southeast. The secondary objective of organic growth from existing audiences in the northeast (by connecting them with financial advisors) would be better achieved at this time not through paid media, but by having the bank communicate the extensive benefits of working with an advisor, directly with select mass affluent customers, using the bank's owned channels.

In the southeast, we are trying to move from Youth status into Alpha status and avoid stagnation, or worse, skipping directly to the dreaded Old Dog territory. As Newbury Bank moves towards a consistent Alpha position, the gap in brand life stages will close.

Remember how successful Alpha brands behave? They:

- stay relevant to changing consumer attitudes and behaviors by constantly tracking cultural, consumer, and competitive shifts

- continue to appeal to new target audiences, while retaining existing ones—but know when to let go of old audiences who are holding back the brand

- continue to invest in relevant advertising and communications that affirm brand leadership

Cultural Analysis

Alpha brands don't look for "white space" in a crowded category. They rise above, as a leader should. To do so, as you recall from Chapter 6, we start with examining cultural shifts. What relevant shifts can the brand link itself to? By riding a cultural collision for all it's worth, an Alpha brand forces others to recalibrate—to follow the leader.

Newbury Bank is in a unique situation. In 2020, we experienced a significant economic downturn, as most of the world struggled with the COVID-19 pandemic. While the markets have been inexplicably strong, unemployment is higher than anyone has experienced in living memory, affecting front-line and management-level workers as industries, such as restaurant, travel, hospitality, and automotive, grind to a halt. Stores are closing because they cannot afford to pay their rents, and main streets have changed beyond recognition. The luckiest among us have kept our jobs, but many have been furloughed (a word few of us knew before this) or switched to part-time roles. Millions are facing long-term unemployment. If that were not enough, in the summer of 2020, historic numbers of people took to the streets to protest appalling police brutality against the Black community.

In the early days of COVID-19, we woke up in the morning and wondered if all of this was real. But one look out the window at all of the masked faces, and we are painfully reminded that this is very real.

Each generation usually experiences one traumatic cultural event in a lifetime. Gen Xers and boomers, who own most of the wealth in this country, have lived through three crises to date: September 11, the Great Recession of 2008–09, and now this.

These are unusual times, and key cultural collisions are, therefore, unique and extreme. There is no question that the primary sentiments in this country are *confusion, uncertainty,* and *fear.* And lots of it. This is the real competition—not other banks.

What role can Newbury Bank play amid these crises? Going out there to speak about low annual percentage rates (or APRs) and amazing new credit card deals would seem crass and tone deaf. Competitors are sending out messages that speak of "unprecedented times" and how "we're all in this together," because this could be our "new normal." Consumers understand that these generic messages of support and condolence are well meaning, but they are sick and tired of them. This is the new category convention we need to rise above.

The advertising industry always has to anticipate what consumers are going to want to hear not at that moment in time, but instead at the time of the campaign launch, which is typically several months after a creative campaign has been agreed upon. Under normal circumstances, that isn't too difficult to imagine. But now? It is incredibly tricky. If you get it wrong, it could backfire irreparably. If you keep silent, people will forever remember that you are one of those brands that said nothing and did nothing.

If you get it right, people will for months and years to come remember you as the brand that not only demonstrated deep empathy, but, critically, that also took appropriate action. The only way to get it right is to talk to people to understand what is going on in their minds and their lives.

Time to set up some research and complete it quickly, before it is irrelevant.

Consumer Analysis

First, establish who your key target audience is. If you are lucky, your client will have a recent segmentation study that gives you all the data you need. If not, you and your client will have to use other resources.

Since you're focused on prospects in the southeast and have a limited media budget, you may decide it makes the most sense to target the lowest-hanging fruit: a look-alike audience. In other words: an audience in the southeast that matches your best customers in the northeast.

Ask Newbury Bank if they can (legally) share any proprietary research data (not private account information) on who their best customers are. If they can't, use syndicated resources to find their customers and examine their profiles. This is less accurate, but you would need to cross-tab the demographics data with psychographics and behavioral data. Look for areas of opportunities where customers overindex significantly, compared to the general population. In this case, it may be that Newbury Bank customers overindex on statements that suggest that they are hard workers, ambitious, and on an upward financial trajectory, such as "I consider my work to be a career, not a job" or even "I am motivated to face challenges" and "I don't like to be in debt." In terms of financial knowledge, they may need help and could overindex on statements like, "I often ask for advice from others when it comes to financial products." You are looking for statements that can identify those who will be high-quality leads for the bank. Note that with 2020 unemployment rates, even those who are typically in a career and who are on an upward trajectory may be temporarily out of a job—do not exclude them.

Let's assume that your client already has the relevant data, and you learn that their best customers are aged 25–59, with a Millennial core. This is the clientele most likely to have more than one account (and who are more or less in the black each month) and have another service with the bank, such as a mortgage or loan. They are evenly split, male to female, and their ethnicity indexes very close to national averages. Their household income is at least $75,000, and their individual income is over $50,000. Most are working full time (remember, they are hard workers—their job is very important to them) and are homeowners.

At this point, you will also have a good sense of who to target: those customers in the southeast who have the same demographic, psychographic, and behavioral profile as your best existing customers, but who do not currently have an account with Newbury Bank.

Armed with all this information, you then need to validate what you have learned and expand on it by talking to both prospective and existing customers. For existing customers, quantitative research is probably the way to go. Set up a basic questionnaire, advise your client that a link to a survey is coming, but hold off sending it until you do the next part: the qualitative research (as discussed in Chapter 5), which will give you deeper insight into how customers and prospects are feeling, and how Newbury Bank can appropriately communicate with them. Only after you have completed this, as well as the stakeholder interviews mentioned above, will you know the questions to ask in your quantitative survey.

While you are recruiting for your qualitative research and preparing your survey questionnaire, work with your team to do some social listening. It is essential when culture is shifting at such a rapid pace. What are people saying? What are the most popular search terms right now? What videos are people searching for on YouTube? What are the conversations on Facebook and Twitter, and what videos and images are popular on Instagram and TikTok? What are Newbury Bank's customers posting on the bank's social sites? How do they feel about Newbury Bank right now? Immerse yourself in all of this information. Get smart, fast.

Now you're ready for the qualitative. Ideally, you would talk to people in small groups or 1:1, but you can't do focus groups or 1:1s or even ethnographies during a pandemic, so Zoom groups it is. Online focus groups are not new, but Zoom groups became mainstream very quickly in 2020. We have all learned how to use Zoom, Microsoft Teams, and Webex. Chatting with your friends, family, and colleagues while looking at their faces in little boxes stacked next to one another is becoming the norm, rather than the exception, today. Likely this way of connecting will be here to stay, in some shape or form, as working from home in the future (at least some of the time) becomes the norm for many.

Online focus groups are much like traditional groups. Even if the video is glitchy, because people are in their own homes they tend to be more relaxed and authentic. You will need to recruit those who are considering opening a new bank account or finding a financial advisor within the next 4–6 months. It could be a change of banks or the addition of a new account. They can be bank, building society, or credit union customers. It's all good insight. Ordinarily, you would look for those who are working or stay-at-home parents, but because of the unemployment rate, recruitment should include a percentage of people who have lost their jobs because of COVID-19. Also try to recruit some current Newbury Bank customers. Privacy laws forbid you from getting their contact data from the client, but you can try to capture some customers through your bank research recruitment.

With your groups all set up, you need to write your discussion guide, a list of questions that will do exactly that: guide the conversation. It is not a to-do list that must be checked off in rote fashion. You do not want to veer respondents away from a great discussion because it isn't following your guide. Instead, go with it—that discussion will be much more useful. (That is, unless they *really* move off course and start talking about what TV shows to binge-watch—which we can all relate to at present.)

Open with a hot start, as suggested earlier in this book—no niceties. Ask questions like:

- What is the most painful thing that is going on in your life, your job, with your family?

- What are the joys?

- What do you need from *any* brand right now?

- How can any kind of financial institute help?

- What is the best thing a bank with advisors could do for you?

- What is the worst they could do?

- How do you expect banks to behave right now?

- What kind of bank brands are you interested in? Why?

- Which are you disinterested in? Why?

- What event or otherwise would trigger you to switch financial institutions?

- How would you go about exploring options?

- What would the deciding factors be: location, shared values, offers, recommendations, number of ATMs, advisors, something else?

Remember, you are looking for deep insight. Continually ask "Why is that?" or "How does that make you feel?" Be sure to encourage those who are quiet to speak up and politely silence those who talk too much (there is always at least one, and if left to their own devices, they can influence everyone else's opinions). Watch out for body language, no matter how subtle. I know it sounds like therapy—in some ways it is.

Let's assume you learned the following in your research. (The facts below are informed by real research my team has recently completed, so there is genuine, real-time insight here.) We'll start with the end of the discussion guide first—the rational decision-making process—then get into the true, emotional insight.

On banking in general:

- there are many triggers for a change of or addition of a bank account, including a job change, relocation, marriage, divorce, starting a business, to name just a few

- people choose banks mostly based on reputation, recommendation from friends and family, and for older consumers, the proximity of branches

- for younger consumers, in these days of Zelle, PayPal, and Venmo, location is of little importance, but the mobile experience is key

- for audiences with family members living in other countries, Hispanic people, in particular, the ability to transfer money abroad for a low price is key

- COVID-19 has made many people's relationship with their bank fraught with anxiety. As banks frantically tried to adjust to the dramatic changes in people's financial lives, many stumbled, and as a result, many people are looking to make a switch.

On the pandemic and cultural climate:

- people of all genders, ethnicities, and income levels are frightened—especially those who are now unemployed due to COVID-19 and those with children. Until early 2020, many were enjoying a growing retirement or savings plan, and full employment, with promising prospects. Life was good. Then everything changed in a heartbeat.

- some homeowners are not able to make their mortgage payments. Others cannot pay the rent and have moved in with their parents or other family members.

- even those who are working feel insecure. Their jobs could disappear overnight, if things continue to look bleak.

- some people are embarrassed and even ashamed that they are in this situation, even though none are at fault here. They feel they have let their families, and, in particular, their children, down.

- people are confused. Why are the markets so strong? Why is unemployment so high when many companies are hiring hundreds of thousands of people, but in different types of roles than before, such as deliveries or online retail?

- what about hugs and handshakes? Will people ever touch one another again? What will that do to us?

- everyone is wondering what the future will hold. Will things return to normal, or, more likely, is society forever changed?

On brands and banks today:

- people want brands to take a stand against racial discrimination

- people are tired of brands that signal empathy but do nothing—those who do take action are appreciated and valued, and will win their trust and respect

- banks were considered demonic back in 2008–09, but this time the economic issues are not their fault. We all opted for economic meltdown to save lives. How could we have chosen any differently?

- banks need to advocate for people who are hurting and need help. If they have lost their jobs, they need banks to help put loans, mortgages, and other monthly payments on pause for several months—and/or they may need a loan to tide them over.

· people need guidance in the decisions they face; for example, should they cash in their 401(k) to cover costs?

· people associate financial advisors with rich, entitled people with long-term investments, not people like them, who need help now

This sounds like a very sad song. So, you will need to probe for the positives in this situation—every crisis, no matter how painful, yields something positive or reaffirming. For example:

· families, couples, and friends are spending more time doing things together, like talking, cooking, playing, or just hanging out—being stuck at home has brought people closer

· knowing someone who died of COVID-19 has reminded people of their fragility and mortality, which, in turn, has encouraged intro-spection and reevaluation of priorities

· it has given everyone a lot of time to think about their lives—if and when things get back to some kind of normal, most people do not want to live the same type of life as before

· for those who worked casually, many want a more stable job

· for those who lacked ambition, many want to further educate themselves

· for people who worked long hours in the pursuit of more status and money, many want a simpler lifestyle, where they work less and care less about the paycheck

· those who overstretched themselves financially want to get back on track and live within their means, which may mean selling a home, a car, or other assets

· all those who worked in offices want to continue to work at home, at least some of the time

They say you should never put a good crisis to waste. This pandemic, the social unrest, and the huge financial strain have caused people to reprioritize their lives, to focus on what is truly important. They have had a taste of a different way of doing things and most do not want to go back to their old lifestyles. The clarity and perspective many people have gained is the best thing to have come from this awful crisis.

At this point, you may be thinking this all sounds about right (or not), but wondering what on earth does this have to do with Newbury Bank, strategic planning, and advertising?

Everything. Advertising needs to engage people or it is ignored. No one is sitting at home waiting for your campaign idea. You can only connect with your consumer when you know them on a profound level—and can demonstrate that and offer something beneficial. You must dig below the surface, then come back up to the level that you feel is appropriate for advertising your brand, without coming across as pandering, self-serving, or irrelevant.

The qualitative research with consumers in your groups has taught you the cultural shifts that are most relevant to Newbury Bank. Some themes are emerging. Now you know that to position themselves for success, Newbury Bank needs to:

- demonstrate that they put people first

- be seen as empathetic (but not benign or syrupy)

- understand the strain people are under

- be known to be genuinely helpful

- be aware of how life's priorities have changed for everyone

- be mindful of the financial consequences of any life change

The strategic direction for Newbury Bank is becoming clearer. At this point, you could start to put together what I call an "80 percent creative brief."

The 80 Percent Brief

This is a draft of the creative brief that is not fully baked but incorporates a clear sense of where the strategy is going. The 80 percent brief saves time. Even if you need to do more research, you can give the creatives this early brief so they can begin working, relatively confident that the brief will not change a lot. Another benefit is that the writing of it will expose any knowledge or logic gaps, which you can fill by looking for further insights in the qualitative research and address in the quantitative survey for existing consumer and prospective consumers (the shape of which, as you may recall, will be informed by the qualitative research).

If you are not 80 percent sure about the strategy, hold off until you have further clarity from additional research. You need to strike a balance: you do not want to waste creative resources or time, nor do you want to rob creatives of development time by making them wait for endless rounds of research or unnecessary "brief tweaking." Don't be a creative time thief. Your account team should have created a timing plan that will help you find this balance.

At this stage, we know enough to put together an 80 percent brief for Newbury Bank. We know our objectives, we know the business problem, we understand what success will look like, who we are targeting and why, and what we want to say to them. Follow the format I outlined in Chapter 7, and your story should hang together.

A working single strategic thought for the 80 percent brief could be:

Newbury Bank. A national, community-based bank that guides people through the many changes in their lives.

It is too long and has too many individual ideas for the final brief but it's in the right ballpark. You can use it to brief the creatives, including anyone who will be working on this brief or any extension of it, across social and digital (if your creatives are not yet integrated) content and technology. Be sure to invite your media partners, too, and, importantly, include your core team, including key account people and your data/decision science team. You don't want a crowd, but you want all these disciplines represented. They will all work together not just on the brief, but also on filling the gaps along the customer journey map (which you will be starting around now).

Banking is not as exciting as sports brands or alcohol, but to make the briefing as engaging as possible you could walk the creatives through opening an account online, experiencing their mobile app, or, better still (pandemic allowing), go into a branch with them and have a look around. If you are working with current clients (rather than on a pitch), they may be able to prearrange this, including staff you can talk with. At the bank, gather as many materials as you can: brochures, forms, pictures of signage. Share that with the creatives if they are not able to join you in a branch visit. The cultural context is also of extreme importance—talk about that as a team. Make the consumer come alive for them. Show them pictures, mood boards, profiles—anything to make it interesting.

Quantitative Research, Part 1

All the creatives are now up and running with your initial brief, so now it's time to launch your quantitative research. The quantitative survey should be in two parts: one for current customers (give the link to your clients, who will get it into the right hands), and one for prospects who fit the profile, as outlined in your brief.

The results of your stakeholder interviews, social listening, and qualitative research will give shape to your survey questionnaire. The goal is to validate (or otherwise) everything you have learned until this point. Quantitative research is the best way to get information about how your consumer makes decisions along the way, which is critical intel for the development of your customer journey. It is finally time to map out your draft journey.

The Customer Journey Map

As you continue to prepare your research, begin mapping the customer journey with your extended team. This includes your client team; engage them early for the initial draft, preferably in a workshop, using a huge whiteboard. (A journey can take up a whole wall—we have massive wipe-down white walls everywhere in the agency offices for this very purpose.)

The customer journey, informed by your research, helps you understand aspects of consumer behavior, such as:

- how different segments navigate the category
- which triggers move them into the category in the first place
- which brands they begin the journey with
- how they do research along the way
- which other brands make it into the journey, and which fall away
- what drives them to make a decision
- how they experience their choice
- how they share the experience
- the highs and lows they feel as they move through the journey
- what the barriers are to them considering your brand, initially and as they move through the journey
- what makes them continue with your brand, reconsider your brand, or reject your brand at any given point

Armed with the knowledge this mapping generates (or the additional research it prompts), you will be able to pinpoint the moments where the consumer is in danger of falling away, when you need to engage or reengage them with your brand. This influences the media team's decisions about which channels to use, as well as any product ideas, service ideas, customer experience ideas, and, of course, advertising ideas to keep the consumer interested.

You can fine-tune your own approach to journey mapping, but you should always begin by looking at the transaction point, when the consumer has decided to purchase the product or service. This is in the latter half of the journey, and your task is then to work backwards to understand the triggers at the beginning of the journey, when the consumer first enters the category. Following the purchase

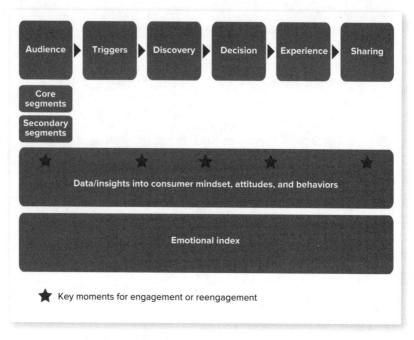

The rough template of a customer journey map, the strategic planner's meta-tool.

point, the journey includes details about how the consumer experiences their choice and how they might share that experience (for better or worse) with others, typically via word of mouth or social media.

The basic sequence and structure of a customer journey map is shown above. As you draft the basic bones of the map, add the data points you've learned from syndicated research, secondary sources, client research, or the social and qualitative research you have just completed. Add as much as you can—try to get close to 60 percent complete—and note your knowledge gaps, which your quantitative survey questionnaire will address.

On the left, place a short profile of the segments you are targeting. There may be more than one audience, and you can have as many as three on a single journey. However, note that each will have slightly different category and brand experience, so you will have to figure out where each audience segment overlaps and separates. If this becomes too complicated, create a different version of the map for each audience.

So, in the case of Newbury Bank, your prospects are identical to your best existing customers. Create a basic profile and identify your priority audiences possibly by cohort. Remember, this is a draft journey—you will be refining all of it when your quantitative research results come in.

Next, establish the key triggers for *your* audience. We have already identified some of them, including a job change or a relocation. Use your survey to establish what the biggest triggers are by asking consumers to rank them in order of importance.

Remember to also ask your survey respondents how they feel when the triggers occur. For example, in the case of a job change, feelings can vary from excitement all the way to hesitation. Capture all of this and add it to your emotional index at the bottom of your map. The index will look like a pulse, with highs and lows, and moments of erraticism.

The triggers section also needs to indicate if your brand comes to mind when your audience experiences a trigger, which you learn from the survey. If your brand comes to mind, great, and find out which other brand the consumer considers, add those, and move on to the next section. If your brand does not come to mind, mark that area as a "key moment" using any relevant and meaningful symbol. In our customer journey example at the end of this chapter, we use a heart symbol. Note that key moments are when consumer engagement or reengagement is needed via advertising, using the correct media channels. In the case of encouraging predisposition and establishing brand credentials, TV, video, and social are, typically, best.

Next is the discovery section. Learn about how your audience searches for the product or service, and, in this case, a new bank or other financial institution. Learn exactly what they do, if possible, and in what order. For example, they may start with an online search for banks in their area, then plug the results into a comparison site. Or they may ask a friend or a family member where they bank. You may want to do some user experience research to establish how consumers search the category and/or how they navigate and feel about individual websites. (The simplest way to do this is to watch people do it and ask them questions as they go, either in person, via computer screen takeover (if they give permission), or via Zoom, Microsoft Teams, etc.) Delve into these questions in your survey and, of course, add whatever information you've gained to date.

The banks that arise during their search are called the consideration set. If your brand is in the set, that's great. You just need to learn about which other brands they considered and why they chose you. If your brand is *not* in the consideration set, that is another key moment. Your client may need to invest in paid search, or they may have to reskin their website to make it more appealing

Next is the decision stage. In your survey, ask consumers to rank the key drivers for decision-making. Again, if you discover that your brand is not one they would consider choosing, you need to find out why. It could be that consumers do not believe the bank shares their values, or they may be aware of Newbury Bank but not familiar enough with the brand to choose it. Or it could be as straightforward as the number of ATMs close to their home.

If there are key moments here where you can influence their decision, make note of them. If there is a lack of familiarity with the brand, for example, but you know that your audience has been looking at your website, you may want to consider retargeting them with messages that will matter to them (such as a reminder of the number of ATMs in their neighborhood). You might also consider out-of-home advertising (billboards and bus shelters, for example) to target them on their commute.

Almost there. You are now at the stage where the consumer is experiencing their brand choice. If your consumer chose you (or are an existing customer), but you know from current customer research that they are having a bad onboarding experience, this is critical information for the bank's customer experience team. In this key moment, you might focus on phone scripts for call centers, or writing a better onboarding e-mail, or on improving the online sign-up experience. It may be that in-branch staff need additional training—information that can be passed on to human resources.

Finally, the sharing stage. You know from your social listening how people feel about Newbury Bank. If they are positive, that's great. Figure out how they can be ambassadors for the brand through an incentivized referral program. If they are negative about the brand, work with the bank's social team to better manage complaints on the key social platforms. If customer service has failed them, and they don't know what else to do, consumers often resort to complaining on social media. The simple act of responding to a negative Twitter post with an invitation to talk to someone at the bank goes a long way. A response that resolves their issue will often result in them taking down the negative post or, at least, sharing their experience with others. The more positive consumers are about their experience with your brand, the more likely they are to recommend it to others, taking you back in a loop to the beginning of the journey and a new set of potential customers.

Quantitative Research, Part 2

You have your 80 percent brief and your 60 percent customer journey. Since you are now clear about your knowledge gaps, it is time to launch your internal and external quantitative research studies.

Let's assume that time has passed and that you now have all of your research reports in hand. You learn that while most employees love working for Newbury Bank, there is a significant difference in attitude between those who work in the northeast and those who work in the southeast. The latter do not have a sense of the brand's purpose and do not feel as strong a bond to the brand. It may become clear that a brand house is needed for Newbury Bank, if one does not already exist, so employees can rally around the North Star of brand purpose and brand mission. This is something you must help develop with the brand team in workshops, soon.

For customers in the southeast, let's assume that when it comes to choosing a bank that their triggers, discovery process, and decision-making process are almost identical to those of your prospects. However, you have also learned that Newbury Bank has a negative reputation among prospects because of its weak website and mobile user experience, poor customer service, and a lack of awareness of the brand's purpose and values.

It is clear that creating a better brand experience both on- and off-line will be a critical step in helping the bank succeed in turning around its reputation in order to encourage prospects to reconsider the bank, and, ultimately, open new accounts. This is something Newbury Bank will have to invest in to get right, by reskinning or totally redesigning their website and app, and through better training of call center and branch employees. You may also need to communicate that Newbury Bank is a family-owned bank that is national, but that has a community-first approach. Your research may have told you that this made prospects feel more affinity towards the brand, because they want to believe that family values will be as important to the bank as they are to themselves.

You will also have learned that for prospects and customers alike, many are experiencing unprecedented difficulties and need more help than they ever have before. Some have lost their jobs, and others are looking for a new direction. Newbury Bank can provide advice and guidance, as well as products and services to help see them through this difficult time.

Refining the Brief and the Journey

At this stage, refine all of the different elements of the brief, including the single idea that is central to the brief. While the strategic planner is responsible for writing the brief, including the final brief, you need input from the whole team, in particular, the creatives, before you go any further. The creatives have been loosely working on your 80 percent brief and will have a strong sense of its strengths and weaknesses. Discuss this with them and refine the brief accordingly. When you rebrief them, they will already be familiar with the contents, which makes things significantly easier.

The single idea in your 80 percent brief was:

Newbury Bank. A national, community-based bank that guides people through the many changes in their lives.

You now know how important that guidance is to consumers and prospects today. They are experiencing tremendous life changes, including some seismic shifts in their priorities. You also know that there is a strong need for a national footprint, but a community-/ family-owned message. Your original single thought was close to the mark, and your new research validated it. Now to make it a bit pithier, add the idea of family (which, in turn, suggests community). For example:

> Newbury Bank. A family-owned, national bank that helps you navigate your changing life priorities.

Adapt your brief to include any validated insights and new learning, as well as your updated single thought. Discuss and validate these changes with your clients, your account teams and media partners, and in particular with your creatives in a rebriefing session.

Refine your customer journey, armed with your new and robust information about the consumer mindset, attitudes, and behaviors. Share this with your clients and extended team for their input before finalizing and designing it. Your final journey may look something like the one created for illustrative purposes on page 163.

Work as a team to discover all of the exciting opportunities that can be created around the "key moments" in the journey that you have identified together.

Congratulations—you and your team have invested the hours and effort into every single phase of the strategic process, from using data to identify what success would look like to obtaining data and insights from primary and secondary research, to inform an inspiring customer journey and creative brief, and every part in between!

Each time you have an internal brand or client meeting, bring out the journey map and use it. Understanding the customer's experience of your category and brand is always going to be of the utmost importance. And as elements begin to change, as they will, refine your journey accordingly or create a new one.

As a modern Super Strategist, you have helped influence ideas that target the right audience, with the right messages, in the right channels, at the right moments of engagement. You can track the success of the work through media-optimization tools, working with your decision science team, media partners, and your clients to establish if your campaign successfully reached the KPIs you all agreed upon in the initial phase of this whole process. You can then use this data and intelligence to optimize future strategies, so that the work becomes stronger and more effective with each passing year.

Now that you have proven you are an essential part of their team, clients will believe that you, your team, and your agency offer them the perfect blend of art and science—and, importantly, that the science part does not dominate the art. We all, in our industry, need to have a creative-first approach. They will feel they can approve bolder ideas, which will not only move the needle, but also make their brands famous. They will trust you with future work, perhaps additional brands or projects to work on, which is incremental revenue for your agency. All of this will ultimately ensure better, longer-term client relationships, as well as the health of the agency.

Your team will trust your smarts and judgment. Your creative partners will have faith in their Super Strategist's ability to help them create the most brilliant, unique ideas their brains and imaginations can muster, knowing that all the groundwork has been done to help these ideas succeed in every single aspect of the word. Let us remind ourselves—why is powerful, groundbreaking, and successful work so important?

Because when the work is good, everything is good.

FACING: A customer journey map incorporates everything a strategic planner learns about the category, brand, and consumer.
* For illustrative purposes only.

NEWBURY BANK CUSTOMER JOURNEY*

Column headers (journey stages): AUDIENCE | TRIGGERS | DISCOVERY | DECISION | EXPERIENCE | SHARING

AUDIENCE

- 20% of consumers likely to open checking account in next year
- 69% of consumers spend 1–2 weeks switching banks

FIRST CHECKING ACCOUNTS ARE KEY
81% of Gen Z, 65% of Millennials, and 39% of Gen X still consider their first checking account bank their primary bank.

DEMOGRAPHICS

CORE

Millennials
Ages 25–39
These consumers are balancing many complex financial priorities as they work towards their goals in life. They are looking for banks with the best value and that can help them prioritize these goals.

SECONDARY

Gen Z
Ages 18–24
Growing up in part in the recession, this generation is trying to establish good financial habits to set themselves up for success (starting saving, wary of debt).

Gen X
Ages 40–59
They are in their peak earning years, and as we are interested in especially the Mass Affluent in this segment, as they are looking for a bank they can trust and rely on as the economy becomes more unstable, along with the job market.

TRIGGERS

- 34% of Gen Z take 1–2 months
- 29% of Millennials do a lot of research

PARENTS PLAYING A GROWING ROLE IN FIRST CHECKING ACCOUNT DECISIONS

First Checking Account Trigger
- A job/salary
- More responsible for money
- Parents opened it
- Save to pay for things
- Going to college

	Z	M	X
A job/salary	37	41	40
More responsible for money	32	27	13
Parents opened it	27	27	30
Save to pay for things	25	22	19

Decision Stakeholders
- I decided with my parents
- I decided on my own
- My parents decided for me

	Z	M	X
I decided with my parents	38	39	21
I decided on my own	36	39	52
My parents decided for me	22	23	10

SWITCHING BANK ACCOUNTS
Customers looking for attractive and useful tools & services

Reason for switch:
- Attractive loyalty program
- Better online banking
- Close to where I lived
- Better tools & services
- Better financial products
- Moved to a new area
- New bank's values
- Negative experience

	Z	M	X
Attractive loyalty program	26	15	4
Better online banking	25	25	17
Close to where I lived	22	20	26
Better tools & services	22	19	11
Better financial products	22	19	13
Moved to a new area	13	16	13
New bank's values	9	20	10
Negative experience	4	18	6

Primary Bank Satisfaction
- Highly satisfied
- Somewhat satisfied

	Z	M	X
Highly satisfied	34	41	50
Somewhat satisfied	32	31	24

Many are only somewhat satisfied with their bank, Gen X more satisfied

DISCOVERY

Reputation and referrals are key

Bank's digital presence & reviews are key to all

WHERE THEY ARE LOOKING

RESEARCH ACTIONS
- Online reviews
- Convenient banks
- eConvenient banks
- Talk friends/coworkers
- Talk family
- Employer/College
- Bank employees

	Z	M	X
Online reviews	40	43	39
Convenient banks	36	34	38
eConvenient banks	35	41	30
Talk friends/coworkers	29	19	12
Talk family	18	12	10
Employer/College	17	16	4
Bank employees	13	17	25

Bank reputation is critical

Loyalty Programs Key for Gen Z

Offers/fees of less importance

WHAT THEY ARE LOOKING FOR

RATIONAL
- Bank reputation
- Mobile banking app
- Online banking
- Customer service
- National bank
- Local bank
- Low/no fees
- Promotional offers
- Nearby ATMs/locations

	Z	M	X
Bank reputation	40	38	34
Mobile banking app	37	42	28
Online banking	33	42	26
Customer service	29	24	15
National bank	21	17	25
Local bank	20	16	17
Low/no fees	14	19	15
Promotional offers	11	22	22
Nearby ATMs/locations	8	16	30

Referrals are crucial to all

RESEARCH INFLUENCES
- Parents
- Family
- Close friends
- Online reviews
- Word of mouth
- Spouse/partner
- Brand advertising
- Offer advertising

	Z	M	X
Parents	45	25	7
Family	31	53	16
Close friends	16	15	8
Online reviews	16	23	18
Word of mouth	16	19	17
Spouse/partner	18	12	9
Brand advertising	13	14	12
Offer advertising	11	13	11

Security matches convenience for young gens

A respectful bank is important to all

EMOTIONAL
- Safe & secure
- Convenient
- Helpful
- Honest
- Respectful
- Transparent
- Customer oriented

	Z	M	X
Safe & secure	44	42	47
Convenient	40	44	33
Helpful	34	34	33
Honest	34	30	27
Respectful	27	26	23
Transparent	22	17	14
Customer oriented	22	29	37

Although 69% of consumers wouldn't open an account with a digital bank, some consumers think digital-only banks are better for savings accounts (41%) & for checking accounts (33%)

Increase consideration for Gen Z: 43% of consumers would consider Newbury Bank for a checking account, but only 37% of Gen Z do

DECISION

59% of consumers have one checking account, 30% have two

WOULD CHOOSE NEW BANK FOR
- Low fees
- Nearby ATMs/locations
- Better interest rates
- Convenient hours
- Customer service
- Bank reputation
- Avoid fees
- Online banking

Low fees	65%
Nearby ATMs/locations	57%
Better interest rates	38%
Convenient hours	37%
Customer service	27%
Bank reputation	25%
Avoid fees	25%
Online banking	24%

While a few of consumers have no worries about opening a new checking account, 20% are worried the bank will try to gouge them with hidden fees

PRIMARY BANK
- Bank of America
- PNC
- TD Bank
- Chase
- Citizens
- Wells Fargo
- Credit union
- Citibank
- Santander
- Capital One

Bank of America	81%
PNC	76%
TD Bank	74%
Chase	71%
Citizens	71%
Wells Fargo	71%
Credit union	58%
Citibank	52%
Santander	51%
Capital One	47%

*Primary banks can vary by market

EXPERIENCE

FOR THEIR PRIMARY BANK

CHECKING & SAVINGS ACCOUNTS LEAD IN USAGE
- Checking account — 64%
- Savings account — 69%
- Online banking — 51%
- Debit card — 48%
- Mobile banking app — 35%
- Credit card — 33%

Gen X going to bank less than we think

FEATURE USAGE

Go to branch for teller	Z	M	X
Every day	8	6	2
Once a week	11	9	12
Once a month	15	15	19
Never do this	20	17	18

Check balance online	Z	M	X
Every day	21	24	18
Once a week	16	19	21
Once a month	13	8	9
Never do this	8	5	12

Check balance on mobile app	Z	M	X
Every day	23	22	16
Once a week	12	16	14
Once a month	12	7	6
Never do this	3	11	34

As consumers are starting to compulsively check digital banking daily, Gen Y still slow to adopt mobile, 34% have never used it

SHARING

BIGGEST FINANCIAL CONCERNS
- Use Facebook
- Use LinkedIn
- Use Twitter
- Read bank content
- Post on bank sites
- Follow banks on social

	Z	M	X
Use Facebook	42	58	82
Use LinkedIn	32	65	85
Use Twitter	30	38	55
Read bank content	3	8	26
Post on bank sites	0	2	4
Follow banks on social	1	7	10

19% of Millennials think cash offer is last good thing they'll get from bank

MOTIVATION TO SWITCH BANKS
- 35% Bank charged new fees
- 34% Moved to a new area
- 26% Great promotion/offer
- 23% Bank made a big mistake
- 18% Better financial products
- 17% Attractive loyalty program
- 15% Nothing
- 13% Better online banking

#1 MOST LIKELY TO OPEN A CHECKING ACCOUNT AT A BANK THAT HAS THE TOP CHARACTERISTICS

	Z	M	X
1. Safe & secure	44	45	58
2. Honest	34	31	38
3. Convenient	28	38	50
4. Well-established	26	26	29
5. Helpful	26	24	24
6. Transparent	26	21	20
7. Customer oriented	22	27	35
8. Easy to do business with	19	33	39
9. Local	17	23	22
10. Friendly	17	23	23
11. Respectful	9	8	5
12. Big			

20% of Gen Z listed "gives back to communities" as a top characteristic in their ideal bank, as opposed to 11% of Millennials and 10% of Gen X

BRAND BARRIERS / DROP-OFF
- Unsatisfied with product
- Another brand product catches their eye

Bottom band — journey sub-stages:

FIGURE OUT THEY WANT TO SWITCH BANKS → OVERWHELMED BY BANK OPTIONS → CHOOSE BANK → USING ACCOUNT

POSITIVE EXPERIENCE / NEGATIVE EXPERIENCE

BARRIERS / DROP-OFF
- 33% think their current bank is good enough
- 28% think it's too much of a hassle to switch banks
- 40% of Gen X are highly unlikely to switch banks

BRAND BARRIERS / DROP-OFF
- Consumers don't see/know brand
- Negative/neutral recommendation
- Brand doesn't have the features they are looking for

BRAND BARRIERS / DROP-OFF
- Bad customer experience

OPPORTUNITIES

EMOTIONAL INDEX: EXCITED / RELAXED / STRESSED

Acknowledgments

WOULD LIKE TO thank every ad person I have ever worked with—for better or worse, each of you has made me a better planner and has made this long ride a whole lot of fun, to boot. I'd also like to thank every client I have helped make magic with or have gone to battle with. Some are mentioned in this book, and some I am actively working with today. Without you, our industry simply would not exist. I would like to thank Douglas Atkin, Mark DiMassimo, and Lance Jensen for their brilliance, their wonderful wit, and their very cool words. Thanks to Chris, Mike, Lara, and Jennifer at Figure 1 for their support and guidance. Thanks to Suzanne Capodanno for tirelessly helping me every day and for giving up much of her own personal time to assist me with some of the important details in this book. Thanks to Lindsay Blanch, my head of decision science, for fact-checking with me, and to Catherine Rosenberg for creating those lovely charts. All my love to my family, Mick, Archie, Iona, Euan, Imogen, and Isobel. I would also like to thank my parents, Helen and Billy, for teaching me the value of hard work and self-discipline. Much love to my brother Billy and to my beloved Aunt Anne and Uncle David. A huge thank-you to my Hill Holliday family and, in particular, to Karen, Chris, Courtney, and Scott—the people I am in the trenches with, but never without grace and humor. A special shout-out to my boss, Karen Kaplan. You are an inspiration. Last, thank you to my outstanding team of Super Strategists, researchers, and analysts. Every day you amaze me.